Mosaic

God is great

First published 2015

ISBN 978 1 78506 219 3

Scripture Union
207–209 Queensway,
Bletchley,
Milton Keynes MK2 2EB
Email: info@scriptureunion.org.uk
Website: www.scriptureunion.org.uk

British Library
Cataloguing-in-Publication Data
A catalogue record for this book is available from the British Library.

Original content from www.lightlive.org
Compiled by Maggie Barfield
Edited by Gemma Willis
Design by kwgraphicdesign
Printed in Malta by Gutenberg Press Ltd

Scripture Union is an international Christian charity working with churches in more than 130 countries.

Prices quoted in this book are correct at time of going to press.

Thank you for purchasing this book. Any profits from this book support SU in England and Wales to bring the good news of Jesus Christ to children, young people and families and to enable them to meet God through the Bible and prayer.

Find out more about our work and how you can get involved at:
www.scriptureunion.org.uk
(England and Wales)
www.suscotland.org.uk (Scotland)
www.suni.org (Northern Ireland)
www.scriptureunion.org (USA)
www.su.org.au (Australia)

Contents

What is *Mosaic*?

Scripture Union has been providing resources for people working with children in church settings for over sixty years.

As times have changed, so have the resources, of course. Where once 'Sunday School' was the highlight of the week for many children, today many other exciting activities compete with the events that churches provide. Where once school life was largely dull and mainly sedentary, today teachers have a vast range of ways of engaging children in the learning process. It is hard now for churches to 'compete' with all the opportunities and activities that fill the twenty-first-century child's life.

Yet Scripture Union still wants children to have the best resources to help them learn about God, decide to follow Jesus and grow in faith. This applies to children in churches both large and small, as well as those who have no contact with churches. We publish a range of resources to equip children's workers, whatever their situation. This includes the *Light* range, which has resources for different age groups from 3 to 14.

You told us...

You have only a few children in your group and you have a wide age range. Maybe there are a 3-year-old, two 7-year-olds, a 10-year-old boy and a couple of girls who will soon be 14. Buying the whole range of *Light* products would be much too expensive and it would be time-consuming to go through each product looking for suitable activities for your session each week. You need a flexible printed product which enables you to choose suitable activities that will work across the age group.

Settings where *Mosaic* works best...

- Many churches begin Sunday worship with all ages together. In other churches, everyone arrives together, but separate into adult and children's groups and meet together again for a final time of worship. *Mosaic* can be used in either of these scenarios when the number of children attending is too small to make the provision of separate age groups practical.
- *Mosaic* could be used where the premises in which children meet are limited so that it is impossible to provide more than one group.
- *Mosaic* would also be useful where there are few adults able to work with the children. (Of course, there should, for reasons of safety and child protection, always be at least two adults with CRB clearance with the children.) In this case, most of the activities can be done together, with separate, targeted activities for younger and older children later in the session.
- *Mosaic* is ideal if you are starting a new children's group and want a simple programme to work with.

How to run a *Mosaic* session

WHAT YOU GET

Mosaic is a flexible resource designed to give you a structured programme.

There are also extra ideas which you can add to suit the time you have available and the group you are leading. Some of the extra resources can be downloaded from the *LightLive* website at www.lightlive.org. But even if you cannot access the website, this book provides all you need for 12 exciting and meaningful sessions.

Introduction

Each series of two to five sessions begins with essential Bible background to the passages you will be using with the children. There is also an important paragraph giving insights into how the series can be tailored to the children in your group.

Core programme

Four activities are provided as the basic template for each session – a way of exploring the Bible, a worship response, and two options which help the group apply the Bible teaching to their own lives.

Extension ideas

Three extension ideas are suggested to provide more targeted activities for younger children (perhaps under-8s) and more challenging things for older children to do (perhaps those aged 10 and over). Obviously, abilities differ and you will have to direct individual children to the activities best suited to them. Fresh ideas are suggested for each session for the series 'Learn and remember' verse.

Case studies

Advice designed to inspire and encourage you in your work – from a writer experienced in working with small churches.

Tips

Helpful advice for working with your mixed-age group can be found in the *Mosaic* clinic.

LightLive

Create a group on *LightLive* online (www.lightlive.org) and you will have access to a huge choice of resources for your group. The database is searchable by topic and Bible passage so that you will never be short of an idea for your group-time or special event!

Helpful resources

Look on page 96 for targeted recommendations of other Scripture Union titles which will supplement your programmes, provide ideas to help your group grow in faith and help you increase your confidence.

Every week online

You can enhance your weekly sessions with downloads including:

- 'Bible story picture': a regular activity for 2–7s (These are also available as photocopiable pages at the end of each session.)
- 'Audio Bible story': a regular audio Bible story for 3–7s
- 'Learn and remember': a PowerPoint of a Bible verse to learn, for 5–11s
- 'Presentation': an activity with animation for 11–14s

SERIES
1

SERIES INTRODUCTION

SOLOMON

The example of Solomon shows us how God can, and will, help us know what to do.

BIBLE BACKGROUND FOR YOU

We all know the importance of living in a loving relationship with God and trying to do as he wants - but we also know that we often get it wrong. The good news is that we are not left to struggle on our own.

Solomon reminds us of what can happen when we start out by going God's way and then decide to go our own way. The detailed plans for building the Temple may seem slightly over the top to us, but the Temple, like the tent before it, was designed as a visual aid to help people understand the holiness of God, the need to approach him in the right way and their responsibility to live as he required. Sadly, Solomon, having started out well and with the visual aid of the Temple always in his view, failed to keep going. His love for foreign women and the worship of their gods led to downfall for him and for the kingdom.

Are we trying to live our lives in the strength of the Spirit, or in our own strength? Is our primary concern to love God and do what he wants, or to satisfy our own interests, or please others around us?

For your small group with a wide age range

In this short series, we discover Solomon building the Temple. We use some of the detail in 1 Kings to show that our attitudes matter as much as our actions. Remember that the children's moral sense is still developing, so avoid imposing an adult understanding of how to live God's way.

Resources for ministry

So, Who is God?

So, who is God? Did he make the world? Where did he come from? Does he ever go to bed? Why do bad things happen to good people? This book will help children (and you!) find the answers to these and many other questions. Using the Bible with integrity to point the way to God and helping readers understand what he means to them, this brilliantly illustrated book contains witty but sensitive cartoons and real-life photos. Containing brain-teasers, memory verses and fascinating facts, this is not just another Bible information book.
£9.99
ISBN 978 1 84427 123 8

Highlights from *LightLive*

Go to the 'Search *LightLive*' tab at www.lightlive.org and enter this session's Bible reference to find:

- 'Audio Bible story': a regular mp3 download for 3–7s
- 'Learn and remember': a PowerPoint of a Bible verse to learn, for 5–11s (see also page 22)
- 'Presentation': an activity with animation for 11–14s

SERIES 1 SOLOMON

SESSION 1

God moves in

Bible:
1 Kings 5–8

Aim: To realise that how we do things is important to God

CORE PROGRAMME

For 3 to 14s

Bible story game

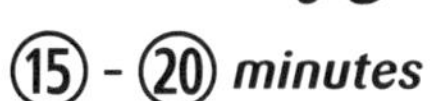
15 - 20 ***minutes***

Why: to realise that how we do things is important to God
With: a dice or slips of paper numbered 1 to 6, pictures from page 8, Bible text from pages 9 and 10, SU *Bible Timeline* or the *Big Bible Storybook Timeline* (see page 96 for details) (all optional)

1 **Set up**
If possible, enlarge the pictures on page 8 to A4 size. Set up your room with pictures 1, 2, 3 and 4 in the four corners. Make a large chalk or masking tape outline in the middle of the room, large enough for everyone to stand inside. Make six copies each of pictures 5, 6, 7 and 8, and use these as stepping stones (or use blank sheets of paper if you are not able to make copies). Lay the copies of picture 5 between pictures 1 and 2, copies of picture 6 between pictures 2 and 3, copies of picture 7 between pictures 3 and 4 and copies of picture 8 from picture 4 to the middle of the room. If you have little space, set up the game as a board game on a large table.

2 **Remember**
Ask the children if they can think of some names of kings in the Bible. Write these on separate sheets of paper and challenge them to put them in order of when the kings ruled. They could use a *Bible Timeline* to help, or use 1 and 2 Kings.

3 **First corner**
Invite the children to stand at the first corner. Explain that today's story will be part of a game. Read or ask some confident readers to read 1 Kings 5:1–6 from the sheets printed or from a child-friendly Bible. Explain that Solomon knew that how we do things is important to God so he started building the Temple in a way God would like. He got excellent wood and paid the workers a good price.

4 **Second corner**
Now invite each child (or group of children) to take it in turns to throw the dice (or pick a slip of paper). Encourage them to move towards the next corner the number of places they have thrown (or picked). When everyone has reached the corner (everyone must stop at each corner, even if they have thrown a higher number), read 1 Kings 5:7–12. Ask the children what Solomon knew was important to God. (*How we do things.*) Ask if they spotted anything Solomon did to make sure the Temple building was as good as it could be for God. (*He made sure the workers had good food.*)

5 **Third corner**
Roll the dice as before and wait for everyone to arrive at the third corner. Read 1 Kings 6:1,7,9,11–14. Ask the children what Solomon knew was important to God. (*How we do things.*) Ask if they spotted anything Solomon did to make sure the Temple building was as good as it could be for God. (*The stones were prepared at the quarry so there wasn't a lot of noise on the site of the Temple.*)

6 **Fourth corner**
Roll the dice as before and wait for everyone to arrive at the fourth corner. Read 1 Kings 6:19–22,38. Ask the children what Solomon knew was important to God. (*How we do things.*) Ask if they spotted anything Solomon did to make sure the Temple building was as good as it could be for God. (*He put very expensive and good quality wood in it, and covered it with gold, and he made sure it was done exactly as God had instructed.*)

Pictures for use with **Bible story game**

Readings 1 for use with **Bible story game**

FIRST CORNER

Read 1 Kings 5:1–6, **then throw the dice to move forward**.

1 King Hiram of Tyre had always been friends with Solomon's father David. When Hiram learned that Solomon was king, he sent some of his officials to meet with Solomon.

2 Solomon sent a message back to Hiram:

3 Remember how my father David wanted to build a temple where the LORD his God could be worshiped? But enemies kept attacking my father's kingdom, and he never had the chance.

4 Now, thanks to the LORD God, there is peace in my kingdom and no trouble or threat of war anywhere.

5 The LORD God promised my father that when his son became king, he would build a temple for worshiping the LORD. So I've decided to do that.

6 I'd like you to have your workers cut down cedar trees in Lebanon for me. I will pay them whatever you say and will even have my workers help them. We both know that your workers are more experienced than anyone else at cutting lumber.

SECOND CORNER

Read 1 Kings 5:7–12, **then throw the dice to move forward**.

7 Hiram was so happy when he heard Solomon's request that he said, "I am grateful that the LORD gave David such a wise son to be king of that great nation!"

8 Then he sent back his answer: I received your message and will give you all the cedar and pine logs you need.

9 My workers will carry them down from Lebanon to the Mediterranean Sea. They will tie the logs together and float them along the coast to wherever you want them. Then they will untie the logs, and your workers can take them from there. To pay for the logs, you can provide the grain I need for my household.

10 Hiram gave Solomon all the cedar and pine logs he needed.

11 In return, Solomon gave Hiram about one hundred twenty-five thousand bushels of wheat and about one thousand one hundred gallons of pure olive oil each year.

12 The LORD kept his promise and made Solomon wise. Hiram and Solomon signed a treaty and never went to war against each other.

THIRD CORNER

Read 1 Kings 6:1,7,9,11–14, **then throw the dice to move forward**.

1 Solomon's workers started building the temple during Ziv, the second month of the year. It had been four years since Solomon became king of Israel, and four hundred eighty years since the people of Israel left Egypt.

7 Solomon did not want the noise of hammers and axes to be heard at the place where the temple was being built. So he had the workers shape the blocks of stone at the quarry.

9 The roof of the temple was made out of beams and cedar boards. The workers finished building the outside of the temple.

11 The LORD told Solomon:

12 If you obey my commands and do what I say, I will keep the promise I made to your father David.

13 I will live among my people Israel in this temple you are building, and I will not desert them.

14 So Solomon's workers finished building the temple.

Readings 2 for use with **Bible story game**

FOURTH CORNER

Read 1 Kings 6:19–22,38, **then throw the dice to move forward**.

19 The sacred chest was kept in the most holy place.

20–22 This room was thirty feet long, thirty feet wide, and thirty feet high, and it was lined with pure gold. There were also gold chains across the front of the most holy place. The inside of the temple, as well as the cedar altar in the most holy place, was covered with gold.

38 Seven years later the workers finished building it during Bul, the eighth month of the year. It was built exactly as it had been planned.

CENTRE OF THE ROOM

Read 1 Kings 8:1–4,10–13.

1,2 The sacred chest had been kept on Mount Zion, also known as the city of David. But Solomon decided to have the chest moved to the temple while everyone was in Jerusalem, celebrating the Festival of Shelters during Ethanim, the seventh month of the year. Solomon called together the important leaders of Israel.

3,4 Then the priests and the Levites carried to the temple the sacred chest, the sacred tent, and the objects used for worship.

10 Suddenly a cloud filled the temple as the priests were leaving the most holy place.

11 The LORD's glory was in the cloud, and the light from it was so bright that the priests could not stay inside to do their work.

12 Then Solomon prayed: "Our LORD, you said that you would live in a dark cloud.

13 Now I have built a glorious temple where you can live forever."

CORE PROGRAMME CONTINUED

7 Into the centre

Roll the dice as before and wait for everyone to arrive in the middle of the room. Read 1 Kings 8:1–4,10–13. Ask the children what Solomon knew was important to God. (*How we do things.*) Ask if they spotted anything Solomon did to make sure the Temple building was as good as it could be for God. (*He included everyone in celebrating its completion, and had the priests take the special sacred chest into the Most Holy Place.*) Challenge the children to tell you what happened and whether or not they think God was pleased with the way Solomon had built the temple. Why?

Imaginative prayer

Why: to think about God being present with us

1 Ask the children to stand in a small circle so that they are almost touching one another.

2 Tell them to imagine that God is standing in the centre of the circle.

3 Ask the children to move out to make space for God in the middle of them.

4 Say that God is awesome – he created the whole world and everything in it! Encourage each child to think of something God has done that shows his power.

5 This awesome God wants to be with us! Ask the children to kneel and privately ask God to help them remember that he is always with them.

Acting

Why: to explore doing things with a good or bad attitude

1 Invite the children to form pairs. Whisper to each pair an action to act out, with one child doing it in a way that would please God, the other in a way that wouldn't. Possible actions could be:

- to tidy your room when you want to be playing;
- to show a new child at school where the toilets are;
- share out the toys with everyone;
- get ready for school;
- get into the car;
- read the Bible;
- get ready for bed.

2 Encourage each pair to 'perform' their actions. Invite the others to guess what they are doing. Challenge them to say who is doing it in a way that pleases God. Help the children find words to describe the attitudes shown, such as selfish, caring, patient, loving and unkind.

Architects

Why: to consider the complexity of Solomon's task
With: art materials

1 Invite the children to create pictures of a building to use for worshipping God. Encourage them to 'think big' and come up with extravagant designs.

2 Admire the finished pictures and then talk about the practicalities: How would they go about building one of these places? Where would they start? What would they need? Realise that it could be complex and difficult!

3 Explain that you will be discovering what it takes to build a Temple as you find out about one of the big tasks God had for King Solomon to do.

EXTENSION IDEAS

Activities for younger children

Mime with instructions

(5) *minutes*

Why: to experience following instructions to build the Temple
With: scroll picture from page 13, Bible

1 Show the children all the instructions in the Bible that God gave Solomon to build the Temple (1 Kings 5–8).

2 Explain to the children that you are going to see if they can follow your instructions to mime building a Temple. Ask them all to stand in a space to begin their mime.

3 Read 'How to build a Temple for God' from page 13. Pause after each point, allowing the children to mime the activity. If they are struggling with their mime, demonstrate examples to help them.

4 When the children have built the Temple, remind them that Solomon followed God's instructions to build the wonderful Temple for God. And they have just followed your instructions!

5 Emphasise that God guided Solomon and showed him what to do. God also wants to guide us and show us what it is best to do.

Bible story picture

Why: to see how God plans, guides and directs what we think and do
With: a copy of the picture on page 14 (printed on A4 paper) for each child or enlarged copies for group use, art and craft materials

1 You can use the picture as an introduction to the Bible story or to help you review the story together.

2 Say that, when Solomon started to build the special building for God, he didn't want it to be messy and noisy! He wanted everything to be peaceful and quiet – no shouting or loud hammering.

3 Look at the picture together and describe what you can see – but remember to speak quietly and not make a lot of noise! Can the children find Solomon? What is he doing? Chat about how well the building is going: do the children think there is much more to do?

4 Allow time for the children to colour their own pictures or work together on an enlarged group scene. Work quietly and carefully, whispering to pass the crayons or comment on what you are doing.

5 Say that, next time, you will be finding out about a very noisy day at the new Temple.

For older children

Creative worship

Why: to give our best to God
With: business-card-sized pieces of card, pens, Bibles

1 Explain that in Romans 12:1,2 it describes worship as service – offering yourself as a living sacrifice. This is because there are two New Testament words for worship, one to do with a special act of reverence and one to do with living day-to-day.

2 Discuss with the young people:
- What is the best you have? A special thing? A special skill?
- How might you worship God with it or incorporate it into worship?

If the skill or possession does not easily fit into an act of worship, ask how the young person might remember to acknowledge God each time they use it or it is seen. How can they remember God with their football skill, culinary expertise or child-minding technique?

3 Give everyone a business-card-sized piece of card and encourage them to write the words of Romans 12:1,2 on one side. On the reverse, ask them to write the following: 'My special skill/thing is...' followed by 'I will offer this to you, Lord.'

4 Encourage them to decorate the cards and take them home as bookmarks.

THE LEARN AND REMEMBER VERSE

'Holy, holy, holy! The Lord Almighty is holy! His glory fills the world.'

Isaiah 6:3

Ask the children what they think the word 'holy' means. Say the verse together, starting off crouched down and gradually standing up and stretching out arms.

Find a poster for this Learn and remember verse on page 22.

You could also use the song 'Holy', on the *Bitesize Bible Songs 2* CD, available from Scripture Union.

Scroll for use with **Mime with instructions**

How to build a Temple for God

1. Write a letter to ask for wood for the Temple.
2. Chop down trees for the wood for the Temple.
3. Send the wood to Solomon for the Temple.
4. Find strong men to cut out stone for the Temple.
5. Cut out stone to build the Temple.
6. Build a Temple for God.

Use with **Bible story picture**

Solomon builds for God 1 Kings 5:1 – 6:1

SERIES 1 SOLOMON

SESSION 2

Solomon moves out

Bible:
1 Kings 11:1–13,26–43;
12:1 – 13:10

Aim: To remember that there are consequences if we ignore God

CORE PROGRAMME

For 3 to 14s

Bible story with chant

minutes

Why: to remember that there are consequences if we ignore God
With: labels enlarged from page 16, a simple crown made of card (template on page 17), SU *Bible Timeline* or the *Big Bible Storybook Timeline* (see page 96 for details) (all optional)

1 **Prepare**
In advance, make name labels for David, Jeroboam, Jonathan, Rehoboam, Saul and Solomon. Make a simple crown (use several template pieces, taped together, from page 17).

2 **Remember**
Challenge the children to recall the name of Israel's first king (*Saul*). Encourage them to use a *Bible Timeline*, if you have one.

Choose six children to help you and give each a name label. Involve adults, too, if necessary, to make up the numbers. Invite 'Saul' to stand at the front, wearing the crown. See if the children can remember the name of Saul's most well-known son (*Jonathan*). Ask 'Jonathan' to stand in front of 'Saul'. Explain that King Saul did not go on obeying God. The consequence of this was that, when he died, his son Jonathan did not become king.

Ask who became king instead (*David*). Invite 'David' to stand next to 'Jonathan' and wear the crown. Explain that David kept obeying God. The consequence of this was that when he died, one of his sons became king. Invite 'Solomon' to stand two steps in front of 'David' and wear the crown. Ask the children what they remember about Solomon from the previous session. (*He built the Temple.*)

3 **Guess**
Invite the children to say if they think Solomon would keep on obeying God like his dad, David. Suggest that he might stop obeying God, like the first king, Saul. Challenge them to listen out for what Solomon did and the consequences in today's story.

4 **Mime and chant**
Teach the children two chants:

A: Remember the Lord in everything you do and he will show you the right way.

B: Go this way – go that way – go any way but God's way. Don't worry about the consequences!

Encourage everyone to say the chants when you say 'Remember' or 'Go this way'.

Story: Solomon had been a good and wise king, always following God.

Remember... (*All: 'Remember the Lord in everything you do and he will show you the right way.'*) He married lots of wives who worshipped other gods. They told Solomon to worship other gods.

Go this way... (*All: 'Go this way – go that way – go any way but God's way. Don't worry about the consequences!'*) And Solomon did. He stopped obeying God. So God spoke to him.

Remember... God told him that if he did not obey him, things would go wrong for his son. But Solomon kept listening to his wives instead. When Solomon died, his son, Rehoboam became king. *(Invite 'Rehoboam' to stand two steps in front of 'Solomon' and wear the crown.)* The people of Israel asked Rehoboam if

Names for use with **Bible story with chant**

David
Jeroboam
Jonathan
Rehoboam
Saul
Solomon

Crown template for use with **Bible story with chant**

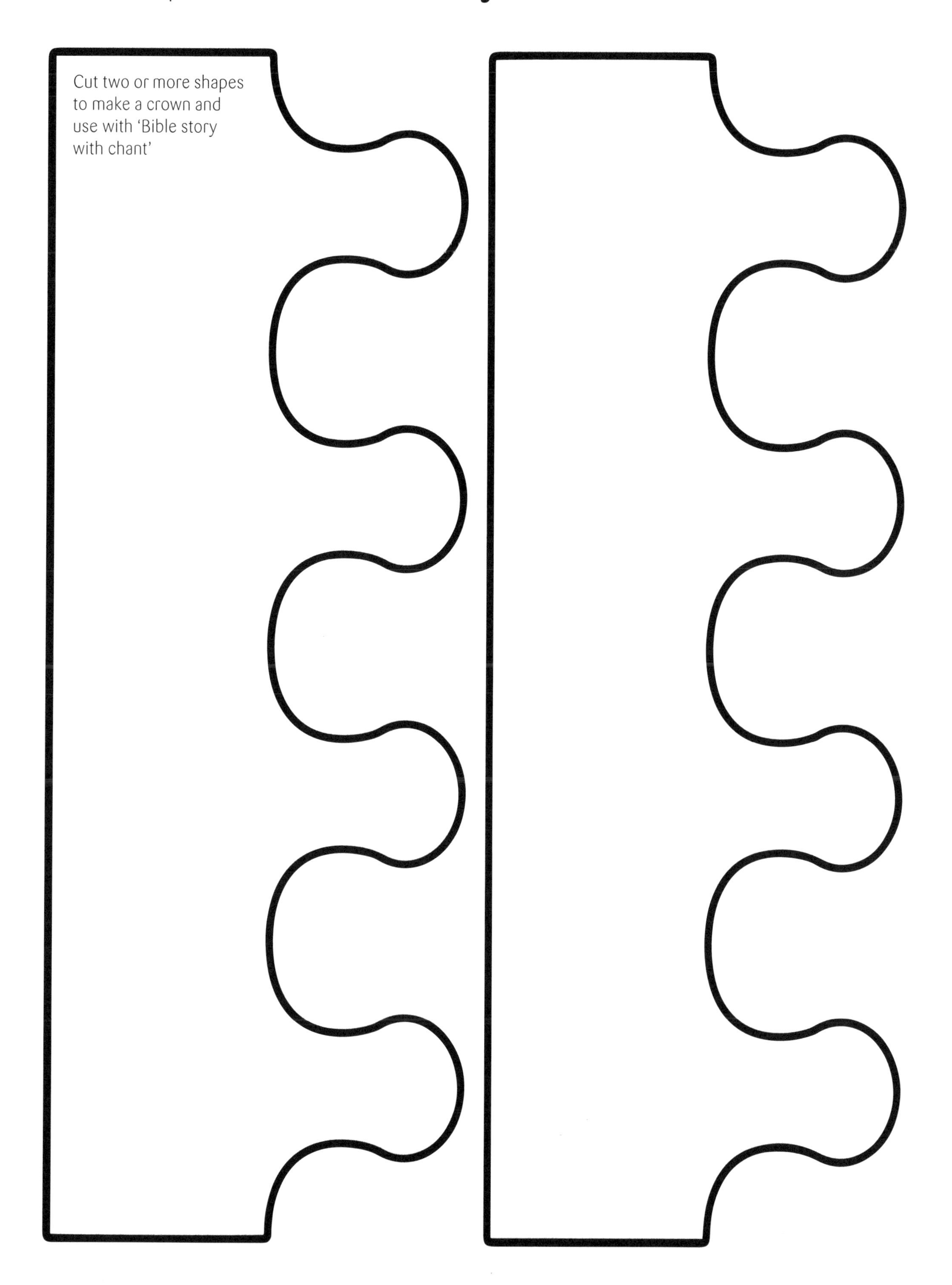

CORE PROGRAMME CONTINUED

he was going to force them to work very hard. Rehoboam asked for advice from his dad's officials. They said, 'Remember...'

Then Rehoboam asked for advice from his mates. They said, 'Go this way...'

Rehoboam told the people he was going to force them to work very hard, and punish them if they didn't! The people said, 'We don't want you as our king.' So Rehoboam was only king over Judah, a small part of the country, just as God had said. The people made Jeroboam king over most of the country. *(Ask 'Jeroboam' to stand next to 'Rehoboam'. Ask 'Rehoboam' to tear the crown into two pieces, one bigger than the other. Tape the pieces together as two smaller crowns and give the larger one to 'Jeroboam' and the smaller one to 'Rehoboam'.)*

5 **Chat**
Ask the children what they think Solomon did and what the consequences were. Challenge them to say whether Solomon was more like Saul or David. Ask what his son, Rehoboam, did. Encourage them to say whether they think this had good or bad consequences, and which king he was most like. Invite the children to decide which chant God would like us to use to help us make choices this week. Say it together a few times.

Collage

Why: to think about the difference between people who are, and are not, faithful to God
With: leaves, tissue paper, psalm from page 19 (optional)

1 Give the children copies of Psalm 1. Read the psalm together. (If you don't have copies of page 19, read it from a Bible.)

2 Working in pairs or all together, create a collage on a large sheet of paper to show the two types of people mentioned in the psalm. Those who trust God are like a healthy tree, while those who aren't are like sawdust blown away by the wind. Suggest that the children use leaves or tissue paper to show the healthy tree standing by a stream, and also show a withered tree whose leaves are blowing away.

3 Talk about how they can be like healthy trees. Ask them to suggest some things that will help them to grow strong for God.

Mistakes

Why: to realise how easy it is to make mistakes

1 With the children in pairs or threes, challenge them to come up with a list of mistakes that could be made in a kitchen. Ask for two dangerous ones, two where something gets broken and two funny ones.

2 Invite the children to compare their ideas. Ask: 'What would be the consequences of these mistakes?'

3 Differentiate between genuine mistakes and things that people choose to do wrong. Admit that we all do wrong things. Explain that sometimes we do things we didn't mean to do, but at other times we deliberately choose to do things that do not please God.

Our code

Why: to realise we can choose how to behave
With: sample code from page 19 (optional)

1 Many children will be familiar with a 'code of conduct' from school. Chat about their experiences. Ask: 'Do you have posters in your classrooms? Do you try to do what the code says?'

2 Suggest you create a simple set of rules for your group, referring to things that God would want us to do, such as 'Be kind with your words and actions'. Aim for no more than five statements.

3 Encourage the children to think about what your group will be like if everyone keeps to the code. Then, with a smile, imagine what would happen if no one kept it!

4 Display a poster of your group code.

Verses for use with **Collage**

Psalm 1:1–4

[1] God blesses those people who refuse evil advice and won't follow sinners or join in sneering at God.

[2] Instead, the Law of the LORD makes them happy, and they think about it day and night.

[3] They are like trees growing beside a stream, trees that produce fruit in season and always have leaves. Those people succeed in everything they do.

[4] That isn't true of those who are evil, because they are like straw blown by the wind.

Sample code for use with **Our code**

OUR CODE

- Listen to each other.
- Take turns.
- Praise each other's ideas.
- Help each other when asked.
- Work and play safely.

EXTENSION IDEAS

Activities for younger children

Searching cartoons

Why: to see that actions have consequences
With: short cartoons and means to show them or copies of a comic

1 Explain that, in today's story, Solomon discovers that his actions have consequences. Ask the children what they think this means, and explain if necessary. Encourage them to try to spot something a cartoon character does that has a consequence, good or bad.

2 Invite the children to read the comics or watch the cartoons.

3 Ask them to give some ideas of the consequences they spotted. Challenge them to spot the action and consequence in today's Bible story.

Bible story picture

Why: to praise and worship God together
With: a copy of the picture from page 21 (printed on A4 paper) for each child or enlarged copies for group use, art and craft materials, praise music and means to play it (optional)

1 You can use the picture as an introduction to the Bible story or to help you review the story together.

2 Ask children who came last time if they can see any change to the picture of the new Temple (the building that Solomon made for God). In today's picture, it is finished.

3 Find Solomon. Last time, he was making sure that everything worked well, for building the Temple. Can the children work out what he is doing this time?

4 Explain that, now the building work is finished, Solomon and the people all want to celebrate. They want to sing and pray to God and say wonderful things about him.

5 Chat about how the children could complete their pictures. The Temple has been covered in gold, so what would it look like? It's a special day for Solomon and the people – so they will be wearing their best clothes.

6 Enhance the mood of celebration by playing praise songs, if available, in the background, while the children work on their pictures.

For older children

Discussion

Why: to live in a holy way because our actions have far-reaching consequences
With: paper, pens, flip-chart paper

1 Hand out paper and pens. Ask everyone to write down their most valued possession.

2 Collect the answers in, number them and read them out. Give everyone more paper and ask them to guess who chose what. Find out the answers and see who got the most correct.

3 Ask the young people how they would feel if their most treasured possession had to be forfeited at the request of their husband/wife/boyfriend/girlfriend, or even best friend.

4 Read 1 Kings 11:1–13. Explain that the passage suggests that anything that stops God from coming first in our lives is idolatry. Solomon was guilty of idolatry even though all he was doing, it appears, was trying to keep his wives and girlfriends happy. He forfeited what should have been his most treasured possession – his relationship with God. It led to the division of his kingdom.

5 Discuss with the young people:
- Do you like, love or worship your most treasured possession?
- Where should the line be drawn?
- In what circumstances might you part with it?

6 Finally, write this unfinished sentence up on the flip chart: 'The best way to be holy with your possessions is to...' How many ways can the young people think of to complete the sentence?

THE LEARN AND REMEMBER VERSE

'Holy, holy, holy! The Lord Almighty is holy! His glory fills the world.'

Isaiah 6:3

Find a poster for this Learn and remember verse on page 22.

Copy each word of the verse on to a separate sheet of card. Make two sets. Divide the children into two teams and see which can put the words into order most quickly.

You could also use the song 'Holy', on the *Bitesize Bible Songs 2* CD, available from Scripture Union.

Use with **Bible story picture**
Solomon praises God 1 Kings 8:1–13,54–66

'Holy, holy, holy! The Lord Almighty is holy! His glory fills the world.'

Isaiah 6:3

SERIES 2

SERIES INTRODUCTION

ELIJAH THE PROPHET

We meet Elijah and find out how God showed his care for him, and continues to show his care for us.

BIBLE BACKGROUND FOR YOU

Elijah lived at a crucial time in the history of Israel, the northern kingdom, following the split after the death of Solomon. Israel has enjoyed a period of relative prosperity, but spiritually things have gone from bad to worse and the worship of God has largely been replaced by the worship of local gods. We first meet Elijah during a time of famine sent by God to call his people back to himself. Cared for in various ways by God during this period, he discovers the faithfulness of God that will strengthen him for the battle that is coming.

The victory on Mount Carmel is a story of the power and glory of God. It demonstrates that he has the power that the local idols lack. But it also shows that a holy God cannot live with rivals - an ever-present challenge. Spiritual highs are often followed by times of flatness, doubt and depression, as Elijah found; but he also discovered the grace of a God who restores. God's power is shown both in displays of power and in quiet words of encouragement. It is also shown in the demand for justice, as we see in the story of Naboth and his vineyard.

Which leaves us asking, how do we experience the power of God in our lives and how will we help those in our groups to see it for themselves? Where have we seen God provide? What do we know of the victorious displays of power or the quiet and gentle restoration? And what are we doing to ensure that God's justice is present in our society?

For your small group with a wide age range

The exciting events of Elijah's life showed God's power, but God is still powerful today. Go to the '*Mosaic* clinic' on page 51 to think more about handling awe and wonder in your group. Encourage the group to look for God at work in their own lives - in ways that may be very different to those of Elijah's, but real all the same. This will probably be in their everyday experience. Session 4 gives an opportunity to be real with the children about times when they feel vulnerable as Elijah did. They need to know that the all-powerful God is with them and may speak 'in a whisper', which is just as meaningful as the dramatic ways in which he sometimes communicates.

Highlights from *LightLive*

Go to the 'Search *LightLive*' tab at www.lightlive.org and enter this session's Bible reference to find:

- 'Audio Bible story': a regular mp3 download for 3–7s
- 'Learn and remember': a PowerPoint of a Bible verse to learn, for 5–11s (see also page 50)
- 'Presentation': an activity with animation for 11–14s

SERIES 2 ELIJAH THE PROPHET

SESSION 1

Power to provide

Bible:
1 Kings 17

Aim: To appreciate the life-giving power of God

CORE PROGRAMME

For 3 to 14s

Bible story with dough

⑮ - ㉚ *minutes*

Why: to appreciate the life-giving power of God
With: SU *Bible Timeline* or the *Big Bible Storybook Timeline* (see page 96 for details), map from page 25, recipe (page 26, also used for 'Bread making') or modelling clay

1 **Prepare**
Make sure the children have clean hands and a clean surface on which to roll out their dough. Be aware of food allergies. Go over safety and hygiene issues before starting the story. (You could use modelling clay as an alternative to real bread dough, if cooking is not feasible.)

2 ***Bible Timeline* and map**
Challenge the children to find the section of the *Bible Timeline* when kings rule God's people. Explain that God's people were divided into two kingdoms. There was a king in Jerusalem and another in Jezreel.

Challenge them to find these places on the map (page 25). Say that Elijah, one of God's messengers, lived in the northern kingdom. (You will need the maps again in Session 3 or, of course, you could make fresh copies then.)

3 **Tell the story**
Give each child a ball of dough.

Story: Elijah had a hard job to do. He was to go to King Ahab and say that God was going to stop any rain falling.

Ask the children to shape a piece of their dough into a man. Ask them to repeat after you: 'This is Elijah who trusted God's power to provide.'

Help them to find Cherith on the map. God told Elijah to go and hide beside the stream. God would send some ravens to feed him.

Show the children how to shape another piece of dough into two ravens. Invite them to repeat after you: 'These are the ravens sent by God, to feed Elijah, who trusted God's power to provide.'

When the stream at Cherith dried up, God sent Elijah to Zarephath. He told Elijah that there would be someone there to help him.

Encourage the children to make a woman. Invite them to repeat after you: 'This is the woman used by God, who sent the ravens to feed Elijah, who trusted God's power to provide.'

The woman who met Elijah at the town gate had only a tiny amount of flour and oil left, so when Elijah asked her for a drink and some food she told him that she and her son would soon starve to death. But Elijah trusted God. Everything would be all right!

Help the children to make two dough jars. Invite them to repeat after you: 'This is the flour and this is the oil that never ran out, for the woman used by God, who sent the ravens to feed Elijah, who trusted God's power to provide.'

Sure enough, for all the time that the rain didn't fall, the woman's flour and oil never ran out. There was always enough to eat! But one day something terrible happened.

Encourage the children to make a child shape. Invite them to repeat after you: 'This is the son who got sick and died, in the house where the flour and oil never ran out, for the woman used by God, who sent the ravens to feed Elijah, who trusted God's power to provide.'

When the woman's son died, Elijah knew that God was powerful enough to make him live again, and God answered Elijah's prayers.

Encourage the children to stand the child shape up. Invite them to repeat after you: 'This is the son, alive again, so he could eat the flour

Map for use with **Bible story with dough**

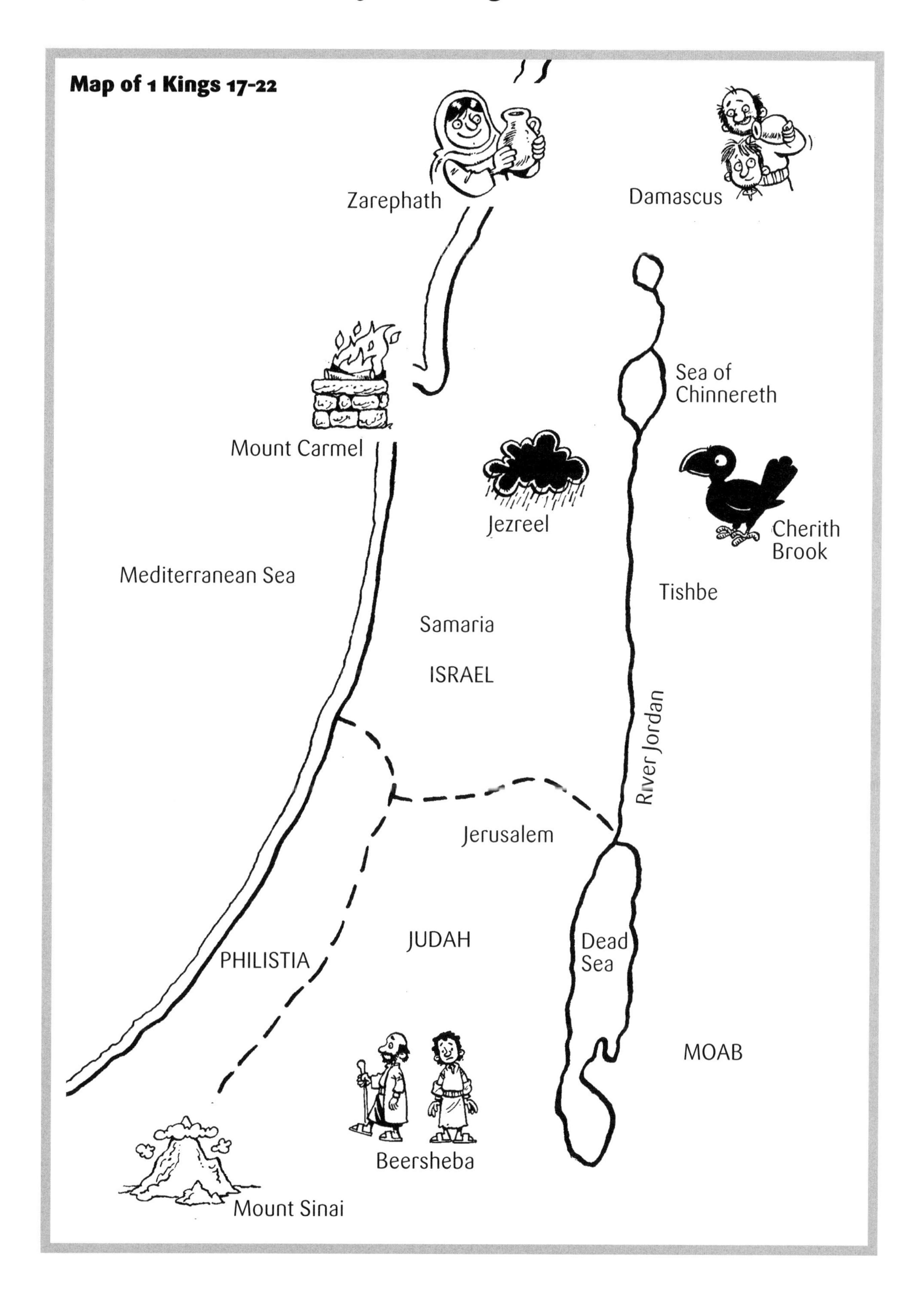

Recipe for use with **Bible story with dough** and **Bread making**

This recipe is for flat bread, which is probably the type that the widow in the story would have cooked. If you are going to use the dough in 'Bread making' you will need to make up a batch beforehand to give time for resting the dough. This quantity is enough for between six and eight children. Alternatively, use a packet of commercial dough mix.

Ingredients:

- 500 g wholewheat flour (or gluten-free flour, if any children have an allergy)
- ½ tsp salt
- 2 tbsp oil
- 200 ml water

Method:

1. Mix the flour and salt in a bowl, stir in the oil and add about three-quarters of the water.
2. Sprinkle on extra water or flour if necessary, to make soft dough that can be kneaded.
3. Knead the mixture well, and then cover it with a damp cloth and leave to rest for an hour.
4. Divide the mixture into portions, rolling out to about ½ cm thick.
5. Cook in a heavy greased pan for about 2 minutes on each side.
6. Eat at once or keep warm until ready to serve.

CORE PROGRAMME CONTINUED

and oil which never ran out, for the woman used by God, who sent the ravens to feed Elijah, who trusted God's power to provide.'

4 **Think and share**
Ask the children to tell the child next to them what they have learned about God from this story.

5 **Cook and enjoy**
If there is time, cook the bread. Otherwise send home instructions and encourage the children to retell the story to their family.

Rhythmic shout

 -  ***minutes***

Why: to remind us to rely on God's power

1 Teach the children the shout below, a line at a time, like an army marching chant:

Even when our life gets tough,
God's power helps us cope with stuff.
It's his power that makes us strong –
Power to show us right from wrong.
Every week, and day, and hour,
God's the one with all the power.

2 Once the children know the chant well, they could take it in turns saying the lines for everyone to repeat.

3 If appropriate, make the chant more personal by changing 'our' to 'my' and 'us' to 'me'.

Activity workshop

Why: to appreciate the life-giving power of God
With: compost, seeds, small flowerpots, a popcorn machine, popping corn, a bowl, clockwork or battery-powered toys

1 Before the session set up some or all of these activities in different areas around the room.

Station 1: Plant a seed, using the compost, seeds and pots.

Station 2: Demonstrate the popcorn machine and make some popcorn together.

Station 3: Wind up or switch on the toys and see what happens.

2 Encourage the children to experience each station, challenging them to think of ways in which God's power is at work in the activity – for example, life and growth in the seeds; heat and energy to make changes; movement and action.

3 Take time to listen and learn what the children in your group think about God: use these insights to help you as you prepare future sessions.

Personal story

 - 

Why: to hear how God's life-giving power is at work today

1 Talk to the children about a time when you have experienced God's life-giving power. This doesn't need to be as dramatic as jars of flour never running out, but could be a time when God supplied an urgent need, or gave you, or someone you were praying for, a great sense of peace. Tell your story simply and sincerely, and it will have a great impact on the children.

2 If you feel unable to do this, is there someone you know who could share with the children? Make sure that they are able to communicate with your age group and that they know the length of time you want them to speak for. Sometimes an interview method is helpful so that you stay in control.

EXTENSION IDEAS

Activities for younger children

Bread making

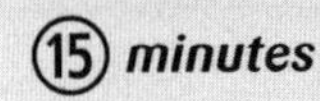

Why: to see how the ingredients for bread combine to provide something necessary for life
With: samples of flour, water, oil, chocolate, fizzy drink, ice cream, crisps and salt or pictures (enlarged) from page 29, recipe from page 26 (optional)

1 Ask the children to arrange the food samples or printed pictures in a vertical line with the ingredient they think is most important for life at the top (be aware of food allergies if using real items). Establish that water, salt, flour and oil are important staple ingredients.

2 Together, make flat bread from these (see recipe on page 26).

3 Make up a prayer together thanking God for providing food.

Bible story pictures

Why: to learn that God is able to provide everything we need and to be encouraged by an example of God's loving care
With: copies of the pictures from page 30 and page 31 (printed on A4 paper) for each child or enlarged copies for group use, art and craft materials

1 You can use the pictures as an introduction to the Bible story or to help you review the story together. There are two pictures available with this session.

2 Ask the children what happens if they want something to drink. They might ask someone; they might have a drink from a bottle or water from a tap; they might pour fruit juice from a jug into a cup.

3 What about when it is time to eat? Does someone cook a meal for them? Do they take a lunch box to nursery or school? Perhaps they like going out for a meal at a restaurant or to family or friends?

4 Comment that none of the children have said they drink water from a river or have their dinner brought by birds! Does that sound like the way to get food and drink?! But that's exactly what happened to someone in the Bible!

5 Give out the picture from page 30 and introduce the children to Elijah. Let them show you where he finds water to drink; and how he gets his food. Why is he eating and drinking in these strange ways? Enjoy the Bible story and find out!

6 Look at the picture from page 31 and sound relieved that, this time, Elijah has found a more usual way of getting bread to eat, except that... (*now, sound mysterious*) this picture shows the last part of the story. Elijah has got bread to eat – but it has still happened in a very strange way!

7 As the children complete their pictures, chat about what happened before this scene.

For older children

Promise box

10 - 15 *minutes*

Why: to remember God's promises to us
With: instructions from page 32 and promise-stars from page 33 for each child

1 Explain that God promised the woman that her jar of oil would not run out before the famine ended. In the same way, God gives us loads of powerful promises to help us!

2 If possible, give each child a copy of the (enlarged) box template from page 32. Help the children to make and decorate their boxes following the instructions. Alternatively you might like to purchase small boxes for the children to decorate from a local craft store.

3 Give each child several star shapes and encourage them to write out some of God's promises on their stars or cut out the promise-stars from page 33. Invite them to put their promise-stars in their box.

4 Encourage the children to take their boxes home, read their promises often and remember God's power is with them!

THE LEARN AND REMEMBER VERSE

'God's Spirit fills us with power, love and self-control.'

2 Timothy 1:7

If you made the 'Promise box' (page 32), remind the children that this is one of the promises in their box. Read the words alternately several times, as follows. Start by saying the first word. Invite everyone to say the second word. You say the third word, they follow with the fourth, and so on. Then swap over so that the children start and you follow.

Find a poster for this Learn and remember verse on page 50.

You could also use the song 'God's Spirit', on the *Bitesize Bible Songs 2* CD, available from Scripture Union.

Pictures for use with **Bread making**

Enlarge these pictures before giving them to the children to arrange.

Use with **Bible story pictures**
God feeds Elijah 1 Kings 17:1–7

Use with **Bible story pictures**
God helps a family 1 Kings 17:8–24

Template for use with **Promise box**

How to make your promise box

1. Enlarge and copy on to thin card if possible.
2. Cut out the box and lid shapes.
3. Fold up the sides of the box and glue tabs in place.
4. Fold down the edges of the lid and glue the tabs in place.
5. Decorate as you wish.
6. Put your promise-stars in your box, and put the lid on.

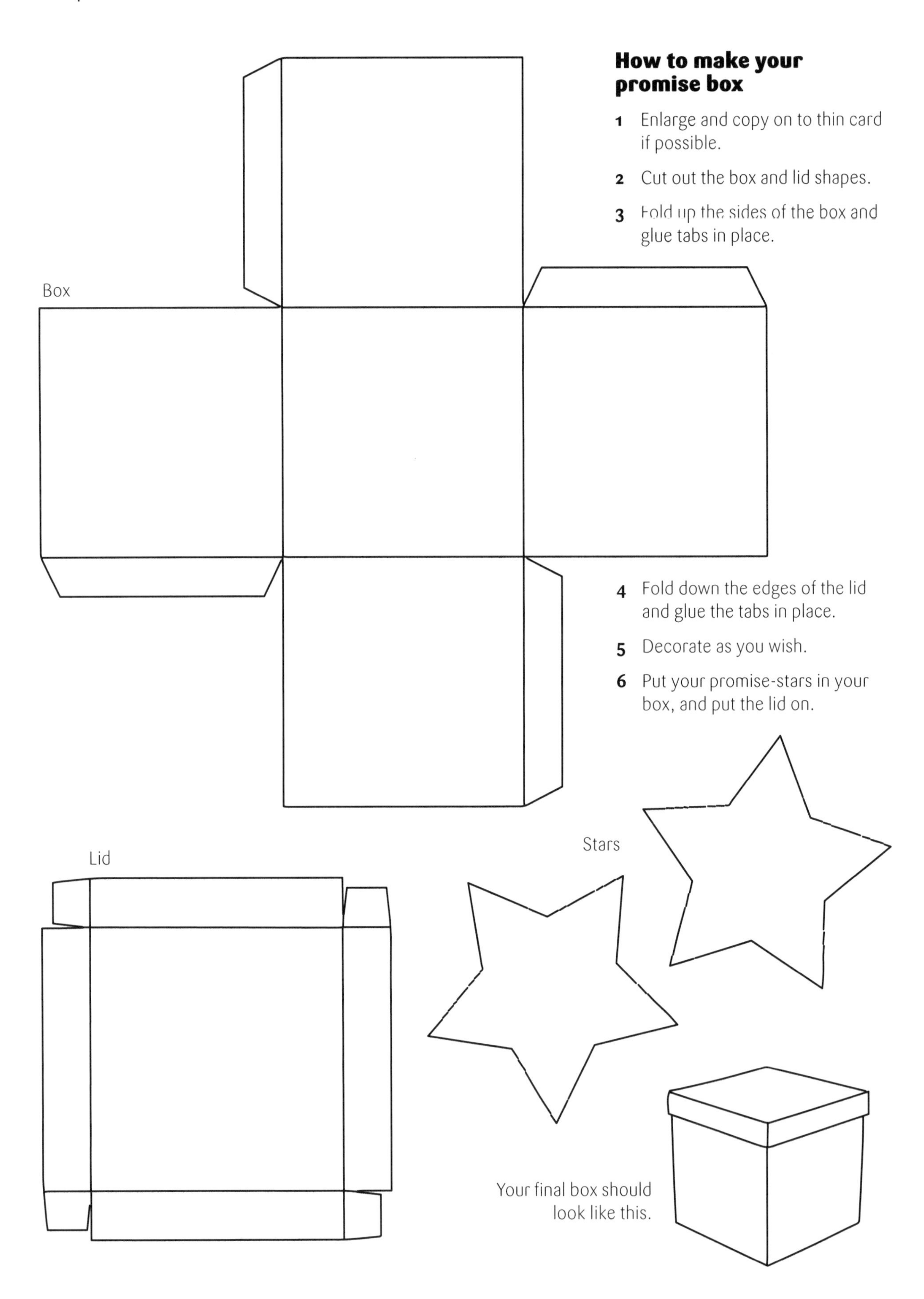

Promise-stars for use with **Promise box**

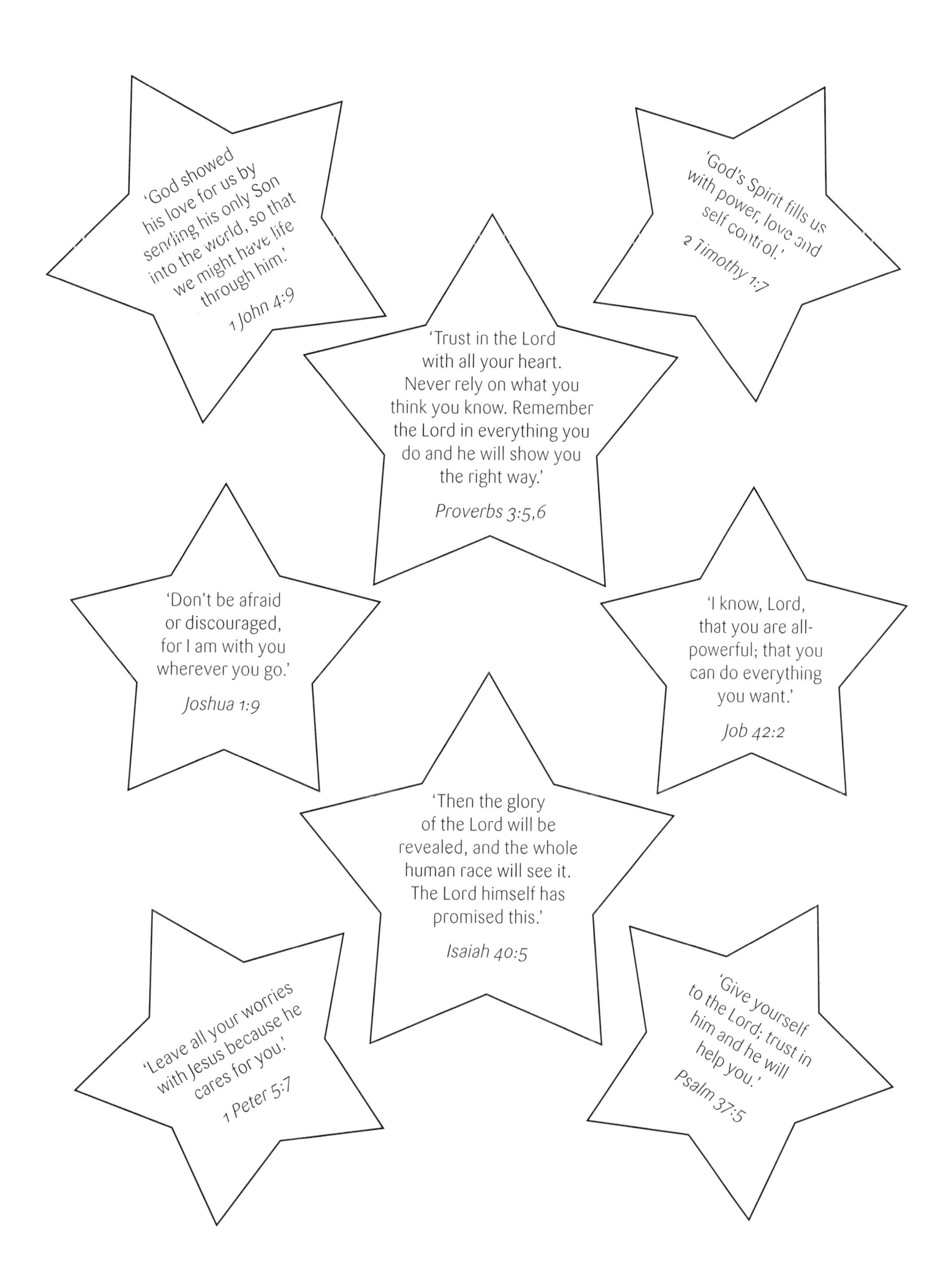

SERIES 2 ELIJAH THE PROPHET

SESSION 2

Power to amaze

Bible:
1 Kings 18

Aim: To recognise God as the one and only all-powerful Lord

CORE PROGRAMME

For 3 to 14s

Bible story and drama

20 - 30 *minutes*

Why: to recognise God as the one all-powerful Lord
With: SU *Bible Timeline* or the *Big Bible Storybook Timeline* (see page 96 for details), a digital camera, three large sheets of paper (all optional)

1 **Preparation**
In advance, make three posters with the words: 'Baal', 'The one all-powerful God' and 'Choose!'
The children will explore this story by producing a series of 'stills' – a piece of action from the story in which the characters are frozen. This can be as simple or elaborate as you want to make it, depending on the time available, your facilities and the size of the group. If you have a digital camera, these stills can be photographed and then printed. (Make sure you have permission to photograph the children.) Not everyone in the group needs to be an actor – you will need ideas people, directors and photographers.

Help the children to think and discuss how they want to interpret the Bible verses, by asking the questions given with each scene description. Some suggestions for stills are given, but the children's ideas will probably be much more inventive!

2 **Act it out**
For each scene, read the verses from a child-friendly Bible and ask the questions. Then get the children to make the 'still'.

Scene 1: SU *Bible Timeline* (if you have one). How could you illustrate where this story comes in the Old Testament?

Suggestion for still: Point to Elijah's name on the *Timeline*.

Scene 2: 1 Kings 18:16b–19. Elijah and Ahab meet.

How is Ahab feeling during this meeting? Is Elijah afraid of Ahab?

Suggestion for still: Ahab scowling and threatening Elijah. Elijah points at Mount Carmel.

Scene 3: 1 Kings 18:20–24. Elijah challenges the people.

(You will need to explain that in those days burning animals on a fire was a way of showing respect to God. It was a bit like giving him a present.) What is the choice that Elijah gives to the people? How would the competition show who is the one all-powerful God?

Suggestion for still: Three children, one holding a poster saying 'Baal', one with a poster saying 'The one all-powerful God' and one in the middle with a poster saying 'Choose!'

Scene 4: 1 Kings 18:25–29. No one's listening!

(You will need to explain that in those days people thought that cutting themselves with swords would make gods listen to them.) What did the people do to make their god listen to them? How did they feel when nothing happened?

Suggestion for still: Children in a circle 'frozen' in frenzied 'begging' shapes.

Scene 5: 1 Kings 18:30–35. Elijah builds an altar.

What would the people watching have thought as they watched Elijah soak the sacrifice with water? What does this action tell us about what Elijah believes about God?

Suggestion for still: Child 'pouring' a bucket while onlookers look amazed.

Scene 6: 1 Kings 18:36,37. Elijah prays.

What is the difference between Elijah's prayer and those of the prophets of Baal? Why did Elijah want God to answer his prayer?

Suggestion for still: Elijah praying.

Scene 7: 1 Kings 18:38,39. People worship the one true God.

Why did the people fall on their knees and worship God when Elijah's prayer was answered?

Suggestion for still: Everyone on their knees to show they are worshipping God.

3 **Response**
Ask the children to freeze into their own 'still' to express how this story makes them feel about God.

Creative prayer

Why: to ask for God's power to work in our lives
With: a parachute (or large piece of fabric)

1 Ask the children to think about situations in their lives where they need God's power to help them, such as making friends with someone who is unpopular or being strong when they are tempted to lose their temper.

2 Invite them to write about or draw the situations they have thought of on sheets of paper. Place the sheets in the centre of the parachute.

3 Say together, 'All-powerful God, hear our prayers!' and toss the prayers into the air.

4 As the prayers fall back into the parachute, say together, 'Thank you, God, that you will help.'

Game

Why: to think about who has power in our lives

1 Put large labels with the numbers '1', '2' and '3' up around the room.

2 Explain that you are going to name three people. Challenge the children to decide which person is the most powerful and run to that person's number. If there is time, allow the children to explain the reasons for their choices as, apart from the last set, there are no right answers. (Take care to involve the younger children in the game, so they don't get swamped by older ones 'knowing the answers' too quickly.)

Set 1: adult, baby, teenager.

Set 2: cleaner, doctor, nurse.

Set 3: teacher, pupil, dinner lady.

Set 4: prime minister, the queen, policeman.

Set 5: Baal, lucky mascot, God.

If you do not have room to run around, give each child a set of numbered labels to hold up.

3 When you come to the final choice, talk about the importance of Christians trusting only in our one all-powerful God.

Portraits

Why: to understand that our all-powerful God is still at work today
With: copies of page 37, SU *Bible Timeline* or the *Big Bible Storybook Timeline* (see page 96 for details) (both optional)

1 Say that, through Elijah, God showed everyone that he is all-powerful. His power is still at work today.

2 Chat together about how God could use us at home, at school and when we are with our friends (although he probably won't ask them to do what Elijah did!).

3 Show the children where to draw a self-portrait on the empty frame (page 37) or give them a sheet of paper. Challenge them to think about whether they want God to use them to show others his power. If you have a *Bible Timeline*, they could add their self-portraits to say that they want God to work with power through them, just as he did through the other people listed.

4 Pray for each child by name.

EXTENSION IDEAS

Activities for younger children

Flame prayers

(5)- (10) ***minutes***

Why: to thank God that he is powerful
With: flame shapes cut from white paper (template on page 36), thick crayons in fire colours (orange, yellow, gold), sticky tack, dark background paper or card, your choice of song, such as 'Our God is a great big God' (Jo and Nigel Hemming copyright © Vineyard Songs 2001)

1 Provide each child with a large flame shape and ask them to colour it to resemble a flame. Remind them that God showed how powerful he was by setting Elijah's altar on fire, even when it was wet. This proved to King Ahab that God was the one true God.

2 Together, thank God that he is a powerful God. Sit in a circle on the floor, with the sheet of dark paper in the centre. One by one, stick the flames to the sheet using the sticky tack. As each child places a flame on the paper, encourage them to say, 'Thank you, God, that you are a powerful God.' If the children are not confident in saying this on their own, say the words together.

3 Sing a song together about God being powerful and able to look after us.

4 You could combine this activity with 'Bible story picture', page 38.

Bible story picture

(5) - (10) ***minutes***

Why: to see the spectacular power of God!
With: a copy of the picture from page 38 (printed on A4 paper) for each child or enlarged copies for group use, art and craft materials

1 You can use the picture as an introduction to the Bible story or to help you review the story together.

2 Let the children decorate their pictures but ask them, as far as feasible for young artists, not to colour the flames of the fire.

3 Give each child a flame-coloured crayon (yellow, red or orange) to hold while you tell the story, briefly, in your own words. When you reach the point where God sends the fire, pause and let the children add big bright flames to their pictures.

4 You could combine this activity with 'Flame prayers', page 35.

For older children

Prayer

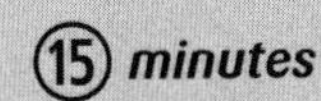

minutes

Why: to pray about serving God
With: a watering can, a pile of twigs, plastic sheeting

1 Make an 'altar' for burning a sacrifice, as Elijah did in the reading today, on the sheeting with the twigs and wood. (Don't burn it unless you can build it outside and in safe conditions. You won't need the plastic sheet if you're burning it!)

2 Ask the group to stand around the altar and pray to God. This first time they should pray that God's power will be at work in their home. This might be a specific situation that they are facing.

3 After a short time of silent prayer, sprinkle some water on to the altar to remind the group that when the water was put on to Elijah's altar it didn't stop God being able to show his power. Likewise, God can use his power for the prayers just prayed.

4 Repeat the prayer and water cycle twice more, once asking for God's power to be at work when they are at school and once for God's power to be at work when they are out with their friends.

5 You could give each young person a twig as a reminder that they have God's power with them.

PHOTOCOPIABLE PART

Template for use with **Flame prayers**

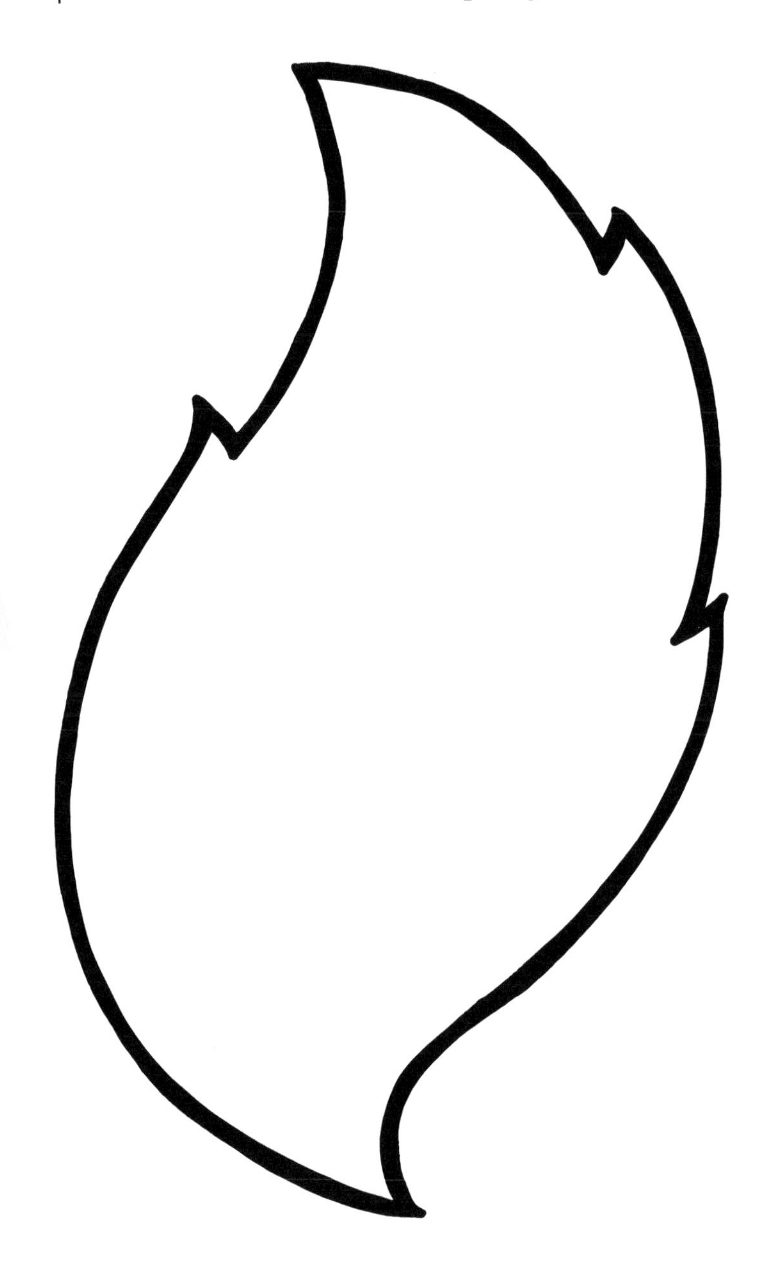

THE LEARN AND REMEMBER VERSE

'God's Spirit fills us with power, love and self-control.'

2 Timothy 1:7

Find a poster for this Learn and remember verse on page 50.

Give each child a copy of the poster and ask them to spread it out in front of them. Challenge them to study it and then close their eyes and say the verse in their head.

Then invite them to open their eyes and check to see if they got it right. Encourage them to take the poster home.

You could also use the song 'God's Spirit', on the *Bitesize Bible Songs 2* CD, available from Scripture Union.

Frame for use with **Portraits**

Use with **Bible story picture**

God shows his power 1 Kings 18

SERIES 2 ELIJAH THE PROPHET

SESSION 3

Power to protect

Bible:
1 Kings 19

Aim: To discover that God's power is at work in us even when we want to give up

CORE PROGRAMME

For 3 to 14s

Let's remember

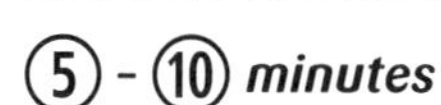

(5) - (10) *minutes*

Why: to remember how God showed his power to Elijah in varied ways
With: maps from page 25 and page 40

1 Before the session cut the 'doors' on the map from page 40 so they can be opened. Attach this over the map from page 25. Make enough copies for one per child.

2 Ask the children to find the Cherith Brook door on the map. Challenge them to say how God showed his power to Elijah there. Invite a child to open the door to see if they are right, and recap that bit of the story (1 Kings 17:1–7).

3 Now do the same with Zarephath (1 Kings 17:8–16).

4 How else did God show his amazing power? If you have used Session 2, can any of the children remember what happened and where? (*Mount Carmel, Jezreel.*) Open the door and review that part of the story of Elijah.

5 Look to see if all the doors have been opened. Beersheba, Mount Sinai and Damascus are still closed: explain that you'll be finding out what is behind these doors in today's Bible story.

Bible story with music

(20) *minutes*

Why: to discover that God's power is at work in us even when we want to give up
With: atmospheric music and the means to play it, maps-with-doors made in 'Let's remember' (from pages 25 and 40), SU *Bible Timeline* or the *Big Bible Storybook Timeline* (see page 96 for details)

1 **Prepare**
Use a piece of music that will help the children grasp the emotion of this story and the power of God with us, even when we want to give up. Beethoven's *Sixth Symphony* ('Pastoral') works well, but other possibilities include: Beethoven's 'Moonlight Sonata'; Tchaikovsky's '1812 Overture'; Norah Jones, 'Come away with me'; *Shrek* soundtrack, 'Hallelujah'; Bonnie Tyler, 'Holding out for a hero'. Familiarise yourself with the Bible passage, the story below and how it links in with the music.

2 **Remember**
Explain that they are going to listen to music that will help them to think about what was happening in today's story of Elijah. See how much of the story so far (1 Kings 17,18) the children can remember with the aid of the map-with-doors and a *Bible Timeline*.

3 **Story**
Play part of the first movement of Beethoven's *Sixth Symphony*, or your alternative piece of music, and begin the story. Get the children to close their eyes and imagine they are with Elijah and his servant. They are frightened Queen Jezebel will kill them. Ask the children to listen to the music and imagine what Elijah and his servant might do now. Explain that they decide to go quickly to Beersheba. The servant stays there, but Elijah walks on for another day into the wilderness. Elijah comes to a large bush and sits under it.

Before playing the next piece of music, allow time for the children to open the Beersheba door on the map. Suggest they look at the picture inside while you play part of the slow (second) movement of Beethoven's *Sixth Symphony* ('By the brook'). Ask the children to imagine what this music suggests Elijah might do now. Say that Elijah wants to give up and die, but God is with him even when he wants to

Map for use with **Let's remember** and **Bible story with music**

You will also need the map from page 25. Cut along the bold lines so you can fold open the doors.

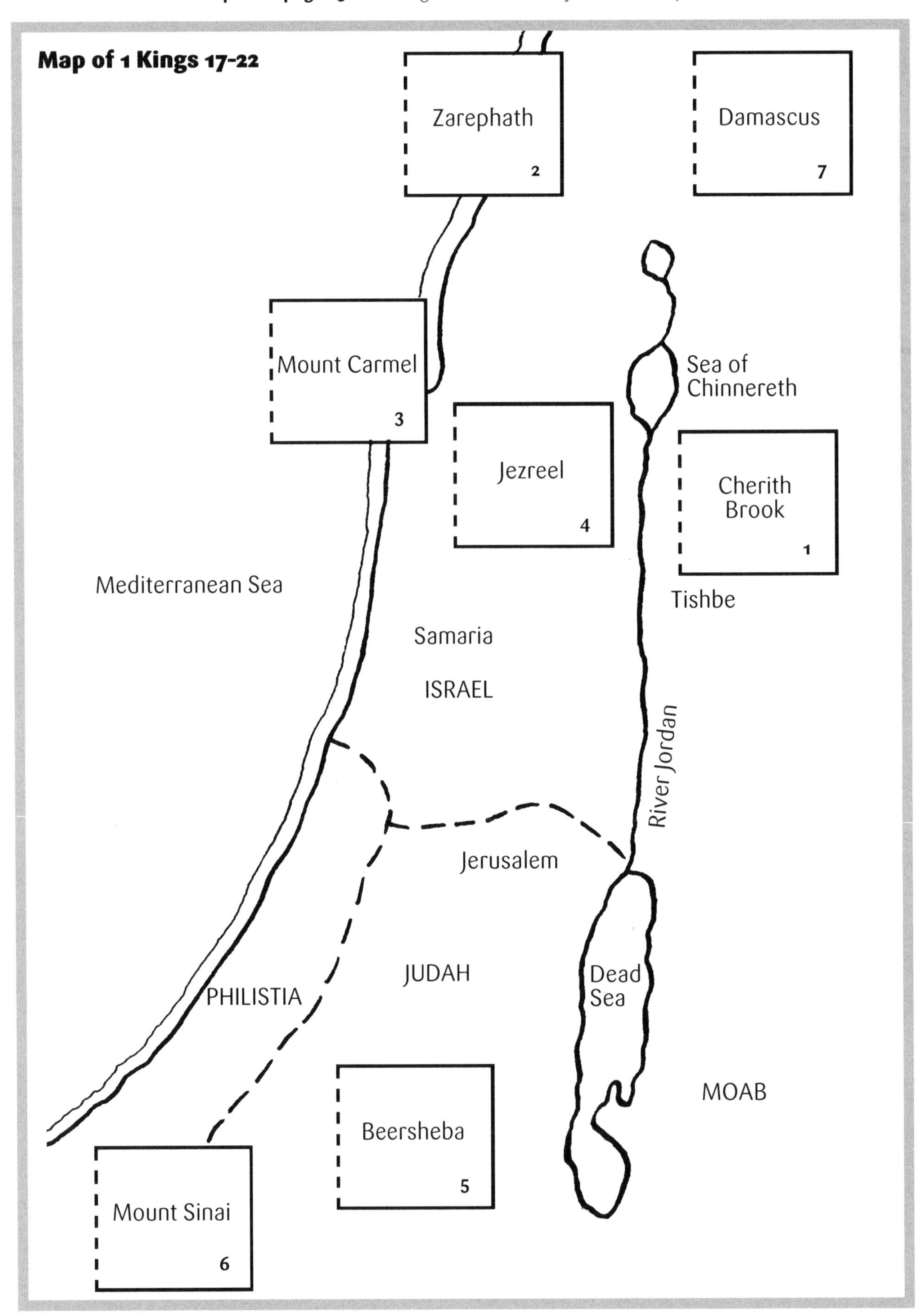

CORE PROGRAMME CONTINUED

give up. God sends his angel to speak to Elijah and gives him bread to eat and water to drink. He tells Elijah to eat it all as he is going on a long walk.

Play part of the first movement again. Explain that Elijah walks and walks until he comes to Mount Sinai, where he finds a cave.

Pause while the children find and open the doors marked Mount Sinai. Suggest they look at the picture while you play part of the second movement again. Ask the children to imagine that Elijah feels very alone. Again God speaks to Elijah. God tells him to go to the top of the mountain where he will show Elijah his power. Ask the children to imagine Elijah climbing the mountain.

Play part of the fourth movement of the *Sixth Symphony* ('The storm'). Encourage the children to imagine they are on the mountain with Elijah and there's a huge storm wind blowing all around them. After a minute, say that now there's an earthquake and the ground is shaking. A minute later, say that the earthquake is gone and now there is a huge fire. Play part of the fifth movement ('Calm after the storm'). Ask the children to imagine they are with Elijah. As the music plays, say that God spoke in a whisper and told Elijah to go to Damascus.

Find the last door on the maps and open 'Damascus', to see the picture inside.

There God would choose new kings, and someone to take over from Elijah. God told Elijah to give his coat to Elisha to show him that he would take over as leader.

4 **Remember**
Play short selections of the different movements. Ask the children what part of the story it reminds them of, how it makes them feel and what they have discovered about God's power. Say that sometimes they might feel like giving up, but they must remember that God's power is always working in them.

Modelling

(10) - (15) ***minutes***

Why: to remind us that God's power is always with us
With: modelling clay or dough

1 Give out the modelling clay or dough and challenge the children each to make a tiny model to remind them of God's power, which they can take around with them. They may choose to make something from the story or something else that reminds them of God's power.

2 Invite each child to show their model to everyone and say, 'This is to remind me that God's power is always with me.'

3 Encourage them to take their models home with them, so that when they feel like giving up they can remember that God's power is always with them.

Pictures and praise

(5) ***minutes***

Why: to praise our powerful God
With: page 42, SU *Bible Timeline* or the *Big Bible Storybook Timeline* (see page 96 for details) (optional)

1 Ask the children to look at the pictures from page 42. Chat about how powerful each person or item is and what they can do.

2 Explain that God is more powerful than any of them. See whether the children know anything that God has done that is more powerful. (They could use the *Bible Timeline* if you have one.)

3 Encourage the children to say short prayers to God, praising him for being more powerful than the things pictured.

Pictures for use with **Pictures and praise**

EXTENSION IDEAS

Activities for younger children

Draw

Why: to think about God's power at work
With: a large sheet of paper

1 Ask the children to draw a big picture together of things in nature that illustrate God's power (for example, a strong wind, an earthquake, fire). As they draw, chat with them about their ideas and why they illustrate God's power.

2 Ask each child to draw themselves somewhere in the big picture, explaining that, in today's Bible story, they'll discover that God's power is at work in us.

Bible story picture

Why: to discover that God gives people things to do
With: a copy of the picture on page 44 (printed on A4 paper) for each child or enlarged copies for group use, art and craft materials, a puppet or teddy wrapped in a blanket and inside a box

1 You can use the picture as an introduction to the Bible story or to help you review the story together.

2 Say that you have brought a toy to show the children today – but it is hiding somewhere. Ask them to help you find it. When they have guessed the box, open it slowly and bring out the wrapped puppet or teddy. Say that the toy is still hiding: perhaps the children could ask it to come out to play? As they do so, remove the blanket and show them the hidden toy.

3 Say that this reminds you of a Bible story. Elijah (the children may remember him from previous sessions) hid from the king and queen who wanted to hurt him. He did not hide in a box! He hid in a cave – but God knew he was there and God called him to come out and talk with him.

4 Give out the Bible story pictures and see Elijah standing at the entrance to the cave. He is still afraid and he is hiding behind his coat! But God talks to him and Elijah does not need to hide any more.

For older children

Map prayers

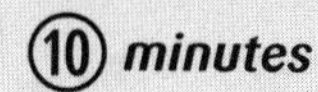

Why: to remember that God's power helps us to live his way

1 Ask the children to draw a simple map, including where they live, their school, where your *Mosaic* group meets and at least two other places they go to.

2 As they draw their maps, chat about things they could do to live for God in each place. Ask them which of these things they might find hard, or be tempted to give up on. As they come up with suggestions, mark them on the map by putting a sign at the place where they want to give up.

3 When each child has at least one 'give up' sign on their map, encourage them to write a prayer on a sticky note and fix it over that place, asking for God's power to help them keep living in a way that pleases him.

THE LEARN AND REMEMBER VERSE

'God's Spirit fills us with power, love and self-control.'

2 Timothy 1:7

Stand in a circle and encourage each person to say one word from the verse in order. The last person should sit down and is 'out'. Repeat this until everyone is out.

Find a poster for this Learn and remember verse on page 50.

You could also use the song 'God's Spirit', on the *Bitesize Bible Songs 2* CD, available from Scripture Union.

Use with **Bible story picture**
God speaks to Elijah 1 Kings 19:1–18

SERIES 2 ELIJAH THE PROPHET

SESSION 4

Power to judge

Bible:
1 Kings 21:1–19; 22:29–40

Aim: To see that even powerful people aren't as powerful as God

CORE PROGRAMME

For 3 to 14s

Bible story with role play

15 - 20 *minutes*

Why: to see that even powerful people aren't as powerful as God
With: words for role play on page 46, SU *Bible Timeline* or the *Big Bible Storybook Timeline* (see page 96 for details) (all optional)

1 ***Bible Timeline***
Challenge the children to see how many examples of God's power they can find on the *Bible Timeline*. Ask them what God's power did, or showed, in each case.

2 **Role play**
Tell the children that they are going to help you tell the story by acting out the most important roles. Divide the children into four groups and practise their parts as follows:

Ahab, king of Israel: Look important and say, 'I am the king. I am so powerful I can do whatever I like.'

Naboth: Look down sadly and say, 'I'm just an ordinary man. I'm not powerful at all.'

Jezebel, the queen and wife of Ahab: Look angry and say, 'He's the king. He can do whatever he wants.'

God (the Lord): Look powerful and say in a loud voice, 'I am all-powerful and can see everything that goes on.'

Words for each of the four parts are available on page 46.

If you have a very small group, just do Ahab and Naboth or alternatively let all the children do all four roles.

3 **Bible story**
Tell the children that they must listen very carefully as you read the story. When they hear 'their' name they must stand up and say their lines.

Read 1 Kings 21:1–7 very slowly, pausing to allow the children to say their parts. (Make sure you explain what a vineyard is.)

Tell the children that Jezebel arranged for some bad men to tell lies about Naboth. The people believed the bad men and took Naboth outside the city and threw stones at him. Poor Naboth was powerless and couldn't stop them. They carried on throwing stones until he was dead. Continue reading from 1 Kings 21:15,16; pause to allow the children to stand up and say their parts.

Ask the children who won in this story. Say that it seems that King Ahab had got what he wanted. Ask the children whether they think there is anyone even more powerful than Ahab. Continue reading 1 Kings 21:17–19, pausing for the children to say their parts. (If you think your group may find it distressing, omit the reference to dogs licking blood. Say instead, 'This is what the Lord says: You too will die.')

Ask the children who they think won in the end. Say that you are going to read a bit further on and find out whether what God said came true. Explain that some time later, Ahab, who was the king of Israel, and Jehoshaphat, the king of Judah, went to war against the king of Syria.

Read 1 Kings 22:30–35, again pausing to let the children play their parts.

4 **Think and pray**
Ask the children what they have learned about God from this story. How does it make them feel?

Explain that God has not changed. He is still powerful and cares about powerless people, including the children. Allow the children time to talk to God about any concerns they may have.

Words for use with **Bible story with role play**

Ahab, king of Israel

"I am the king. I am so powerful I can do whatever I like."

Naboth

"I'm just an ordinary man. I'm not powerful at all."

Jezebel, the queen and wife of Ahab

"He's the king. He can do whatever he wants."

God (the Lord)

"I am all-powerful and can see everything that goes on."

Child shapes for use with **Make and pray**

Enlarge as necessary

CORE PROGRAMME CONTINUED

Map prayer

(10) *minutes*

Why: to pray for powerless people
With: a globe or large map of the world or your country (optional)

1 Remind the children that, in today's story, Naboth was powerless. Explain that today, too, many people are helpless in the face of powerful people or events. Ask the children whether they can think of any such international, national or local powerful events or people – earthquake, war, famine, train crashes, oppressive governments and so on. If you have a map, ask several children to draw a heart on a sticky note and place it on an appropriate place.

2 Say that, just as God cared about what happened to Naboth, he cares about all the people they have mentioned. Encourage each child to choose one situation, stand by the place on the map and pray for the people involved.

Make and pray

(20) *minutes*

Why: to be thankful that God cares for the powerless
With: a large sheet of paper, shapes from page 46, nature or travel magazines

1 Write the word 'GOD' in large bubble writing on the large sheet of paper.

2 Encourage the children to select pictures that demonstrate God's power from the magazines and decorate the letters 'G', 'O' and 'D'.

3 Say that we often feel very small and helpless. Ask the children how what they learned from today's story can help them at such times.

4 Give each child a child-shape and ask them to write their name on it and personalise it, if they wish. Allow the children, one at a time, to stick their figures inside the letters 'O' and 'D'. As they do so, encourage them to thank God for his power.

Mime

(10) *minutes*

Why: to proclaim that even powerful people aren't as powerful as God

1 Remind the children that many people, like Ahab, think that they are powerful and important. Who is even more powerful? Practise the shout, 'Stop! No one is as powerful as God.'

2 Ask for a volunteer and whisper to them a powerful person, such as a king or queen, soldier, famous footballer, rich man counting his money, pop star, president or prime minister. Encourage the volunteer to mime this person, while the other children try to guess who it is.

3 When the children have guessed correctly, comment on why this person thinks they are powerful. Ask the child to continue miming, then get all the others to do the shout. The child miming should then freeze. Repeat with more volunteers.

Pictures for use with **Sort and chat**

EXTENSION IDEAS

Activities for younger children

Praise movements

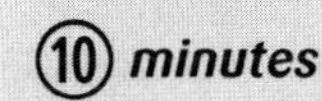

Why: to praise God for being powerful
With: worship music and means to play it

1 Ask the children to make some powerful movements. Admire everyone's ideas.

2 Say that this series on Elijah has been about God being powerful. Ask the children to think of some other words that mean the same as powerful, such as 'strong' or 'mighty'.

3 Sing or play some songs containing these words, making the power movements each time 'power' words are sung. Suitable songs include 'My God is so big' (*kidsource* 255) and 'Oh Lord, you're great' (*kidsource* 270).

Sort and chat

Why: to think about powerful struggles
With: pictures from page 48

1 Ask the children what it means to be powerful. Explain that it doesn't only mean physical power.

2 Show the children each picture in turn and ask them who they think is more powerful in each mini-scene, and why. If you have enough children in your group, you could do this as a team game, with each team having a full set of pictures.

3 Explain that in today's story they will hear about how God is more powerful than even all these powerful people!

There is no 'Bible story picture' activity in this session.

For older children

Share and prayer

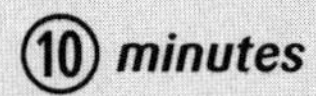

Why: to think about being God's powerful people

1 Ask the children and young people about times when they have to be fair, honest or bring justice. Have they ever stood up to someone who was/is very powerful (for example, someone who is bullying them)?

2 Find out if they can think of a time this week when they will need to be fair, honest, bring justice or stand up to someone.

3 As the children make suggestions, get them to stand up and encourage the group to say to them: 'God is more powerful than anyone and God will be there to help... [*their name*]'.

THE LEARN AND REMEMBER VERSE

'God's spirit fills us with power, love and self-control.'

2 Timothy 1:7

Give each child a card the size of a business card. On it, invite them to draw symbols for spirit, power, love and self-control. Encourage the children to carry these round with them to remind them of the verse.

Find a poster for this Learn and remember verse on page 50.

You could also use the song 'God's Spirit', on the *Bitesize Bible Songs 2* CD, available from Scripture Union.

'God's spirit fills us with power, love and self-control.'

2 Timothy 1:7

Mosaic clinic

Top tips from ministry practitioners to help you make the most of your small group with a wide age range.

HANDLING AWE AND WONDER

Lost in wonder

A well-known hymn speaks of being 'lost in wonder, love and praise' ('Love divine, all loves excelling' by Charles Wesley). Many adults never enter this realm of awe and wonder whereas children are much more likely to inhabit it. I remember a story recounted by a young teacher about a little girl in her reception class who came from a non-church background. She was reading Psalm 23 with her class and asked the children what they thought God was like. One little girl threw up her hands and exclaimed: 'My Jesus!' In a profound moment of revelation, awe and wonder this little girl caught a glimpse of the very nature of God.

The 'wow' factor

I believe every child has the capacity to grasp something of the awe and wonder of God even if they have no religious background or experience. Children are often unable to explain this glimpse of God's wonder and glory in rational words that adults understand. Instead they respond either with a disconnected logic that adults find difficult to follow or in a more physical way, focusing on something beyond the immediate surroundings, gazing into space, jumping or shouting excitedly, gawping in wonder, tearful in joy.

But is this 'wow' factor any less of a spiritual experience? I would suggest not. Adults are so trained in the rational that they often miss these moments of awe and wonder that a child experiences and end up confusing children's experiences of spiritual revelation for a sort of childish distraction and therefore miss the opportunity to encourage and grow their capacity for faith.

'There was a blinding flash of light and Emily aged five rushed into the house shouting: "Mummy, Mummy, God has just taken my picture."' (*Children on the Loose*, Murray Watts, Monarch Books, 2001.)

Created in the image of God

If we are all created in the image of God, then we are all born with the capacity to relate to God. But as babies grow into children, influences around them seep into their lives and affect their capacity and appetite for the spiritual. The rationalistic view of the world, our dependence on information technology and instant visual image and sound all affect a young child and their capacity to relate to God. Over time their capacity for awe and wonder is not so much 'edited out' as choked by the smog of rationalism, scepticism and cynicism about the spiritual. The increasing need for the 'buzz' of new experiences becomes a response of 'so what' to a glorious sunset which children know can be computer-drawn, digitally enhanced and re-edited to make it even more glorious.

But children constantly surprise me with their grasp of the numinous, the depth of their insight, the clarity of their 'seeing' and the integrity of their spiritual responses. As adults we are fast losing this 'yearning' capacity, that children still retain, to reach out beyond themselves to the 'otherness' of God.

'In young spirituality, that passion to reach and affect the entire universe is constantly given expression as children yearn to catch a moment's flicker or glimmer of recognition from even one star...' (*The Spiritual Life of Children*, Robert Coles, HarperCollins, 1990.)

Children and awe and wonder

Children maintain a capacity for awe and wonder that is less affected by the 'seepage' of the rationalist and cynical world around them. However, they are vulnerable to being wounded and abused by the world around them, resulting in their capacity for trust as well as faith being reduced. Yet this is an exciting age group to work with: their enthusiasm for the spiritual is catching; their moments of insight are awesome. If you want to recapture an uncluttered vision of God, go work with children in their early years. Actually, don't – because it comes with a health warning: children are willing to engage with the transformational, so those who lead them need to be open to change.

The key words for encouraging awe and wonder in children are:

- Watch
- Listen
- Encourage

Adults are often too quick to leap in with their 'take' on things, their explanation, their help. Much better to allow the children to haltingly find their words, pictures, movements and sounds to explain how they have experienced, and are experiencing, God.

Offer some experiences. Take them outside on a windy day. Let them feel the wind on their faces and see what affect the wind has on nature and things around them. Listen to them, encourage them to listen to all that they hear around them and start to build a sense of responsibility for the world.

Offer appropriate spaces to be quiet. Create a quiet corner where they can sit and reflect with some appropriate music, a lava lamp or one of those tall lamps with water bubbles rising in them. Use aromatic oils like lavender (calming and soothing), some things that are nice to touch and feel, such as a small wooden holding cross, squares or small cushions of velvet and fur or some cuddly toys. Use this quiet place to reflect on some of the stories and words of God:

- I am the light of the world ... Whoever follows me will have the light of life and will never walk in darkness.' John 8:12
- I will be with you always...' Matthew 28:20
- I call you friends...' John 15:15
- For the Father himself loves you...' John 16:27

Tell awesome stories:

- The story of Moses crossing the Red Sea: Exodus 14:1–29
- The story of Noah's boat and the rainbow: Genesis 6:1 – 9:17
- Jesus calming the storm on the lake: Luke 8:22–25
- Jesus feeding 5,000 people: John 6:1–13
- Jesus healing Jairus' daughter: Mark 5:21–43

These are stories that can be acted out with puppets or with the children taking part.

Have spiritual conversations. Listen to the spiritual in children. Listen to and watch their body language. Give them time to reply in conversation; try not to finish their sentences for them. Be patient and wait for the words to come: sometimes they take a long time to surface.

Above all, **be an encourager**. If children are encouraged, they will take steps of faith with more confidence. If they are not encouraged, it will not rob them of faith because God is bigger than our failings. But it will slow down their growth in faith and disable their discipleship and ability to follow God's ways and trust in his truth.

Rev Jackie Cray
Former President of Scripture Union Council, for England and Wales.

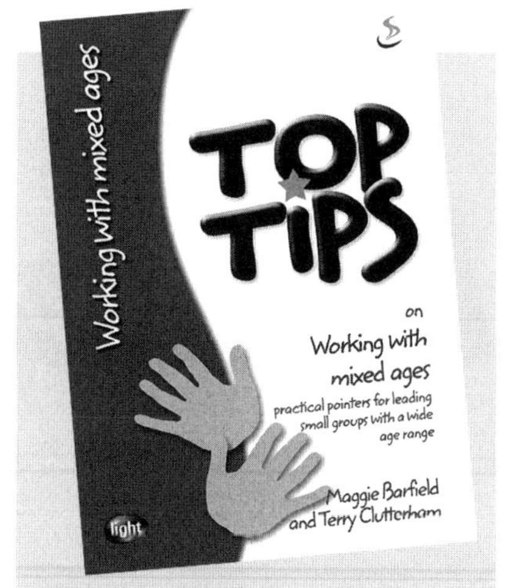

SERIES 3

SERIES INTRODUCTION

JESUS SHOWS GOD'S LOVE

John's Gospel gives a unique portrait of Jesus, helping us encounter and understand his care for each of us

BIBLE BACKGROUND FOR YOU

In this series we look at four very different sections from John's Gospel to see how God's love and care is shown in Jesus. Two are narratives (the wedding at Cana and the raising of Lazarus), one is a record of Jesus' teaching (the Good Shepherd) and the final section is a combination of the two (the feeding of the 5,000). John wants us to understand that, in Jesus, God is doing something new, but that new thing is part of an age-old plan.

The feeding of the 5,000 and the discussion that follows point us back to the provision of manna in the wilderness. The picture of the Good Shepherd picks up an Old Testament picture of God. For John, the whole purpose of Jesus' coming is summed up in John 10:10 – so that we could have real life. Therefore the raising of Lazarus becomes a living demonstration of all that Jesus came to achieve.

The backdrop to all of this is the love that motivates God to act in this way and which has been spelled out in John 3:16. All that Jesus says and does is a working out of this principle. How can we ensure that our words tell and our lives demonstrate to the children in our groups that we believe that God is active in every aspect of life?

For your small group with a wide age range

In this series, your group will be invited to see how Jesus shows us God's love. Challenge older children to reflect on how each week's aim impacts on their own lives. Take care with younger children and do not expect too much. Their thinking is still literal. They may not be able to see how Jesus is 'like a shepherd' if he is not one. Being 'like' for them means being the same in every respect. In Session 4, be sensitive to any children who may be facing a bereavement.

Resources for ministry

Top Tips on Sharing Bible Stories
Jesus told stories to crowds of people. Some understood and responded, some were puzzled and some were offended. That's the effect stories can have! Storytelling is a vital tool for anyone working with children and young people. This book explores what the Bible says about storytelling, presents some basic principles and then gives loads of examples on how to effectively share Bible stories with imagination, enjoyment and impact.
£3.50
ISBN 978 1 84427 328 7

Highlights from *LightLive*

Go to the 'Search *LightLive*' tab at www.lightlive.org and enter this session's Bible reference to find:

- 'Audio Bible story': a regular mp3 download for 3–7s
- 'Learn and remember': a PowerPoint of a Bible verse to learn, for 5–11s (see also page 79)
- 'Presentation': an activity with animation for 11–14s

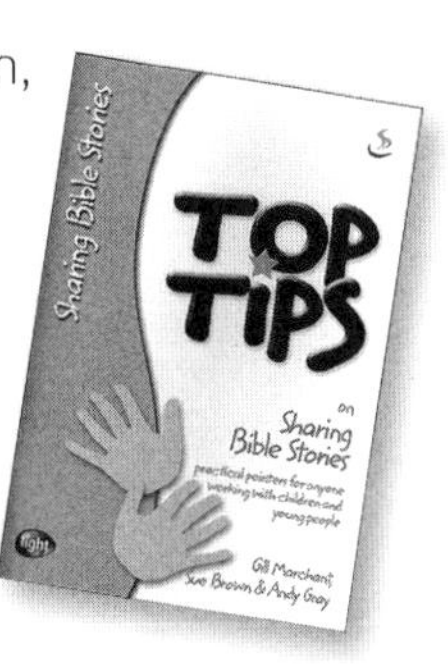

SERIES 3 JESUS SHOWS GOD'S LOVE

SESSION 1

Water into wine

Bible:
John 2:1–11

Aim: To discover that Jesus gives the best

CORE PROGRAMME

For 3 to 14s

Bible story with expressions

(20) *minutes*

Why: to discover that Jesus gives the best
With: squash or juice, paper cups, large sheets of paper, pictures of facial expressions from page 55, SU *Bible Timeline* or the *Big Bible Storybook Timeline* (see page 96 for details), *Light for Everyone* CD (available from Scripture Union) and means to play it (optional)

1 **Background**
Ask if any of the children have been to a wedding. Find out what they know about weddings (such as special things people do, wear and eat).

2 **Drink and think**
Sit together round a table as if at a wedding reception. Start to pour out some squash or juice. (Be aware of allergy and hygiene issues.) Make sure that it runs out before all of the children have had some. Ask those children who didn't receive a drink how they feel about this. Draw facial expressions on a large sheet of paper to represent their answers (refer to the ideas on page 55). Then produce more squash or juice, enough for everyone to have some. Draw their answers again.

3 **Story**
Tell the children that this reminds you of a story about Jesus. Ask if they can find 'Jesus teaches and heals' on the SU *Bible Timeline*. Invite them to listen carefully to the story from the Bible and to think about what the different people in the story might be thinking.

Jesus was invited to a wedding in Cana. His mother, Mary, and some of his friends had been invited too. It was a real celebration. Everything was going well: the bride and groom were so happy, all the relatives were getting on well and the food was delicious. (*Encourage the children to choose facial expressions again that show how the guests, the servants and the bride and groom might be feeling. Draw these on a second large sheet before continuing the story.*)

Then the wine ran out! There was none left! The guests would have to drink water! What a disaster! The special day would be spoiled. (*Invite the children to choose expressions again to describe how the guests, the servants and the bride and groom would be feeling. Draw them on the sheet.*)

But Mary, Jesus' mother, thought: 'Jesus wouldn't want the day to be spoiled! I must tell him about the problem.' So she went and spoke to Jesus. Then she told the servants, 'Do whatever Jesus says.'

At the side of the room were six enormous stone jars. They contained water for people to wash with before the meal. Jesus told the servants to fill the jars up to the brim with fresh water, then take a jugful of the drink to the man in charge of the feast. When the man tasted it, it was wine – and the very best wine at that! The man in charge couldn't believe it – in fact he called the bridegroom and said to him, 'Everyone else serves the best wine first. But you have kept the best wine until now!' (*Ask the children to choose expressions (or suggest new ones) to describe how the guests, the servants and the bride and groom would be feeling now. Draw them on the large sheet.*)

4 **Respond**
On a new sheet of paper, write some words or phrases or draw facial expressions that describe what the children think about Jesus after hearing the story. Explain that Jesus did amazing things because he

Facial expressions for use with **Bible story with expressions**

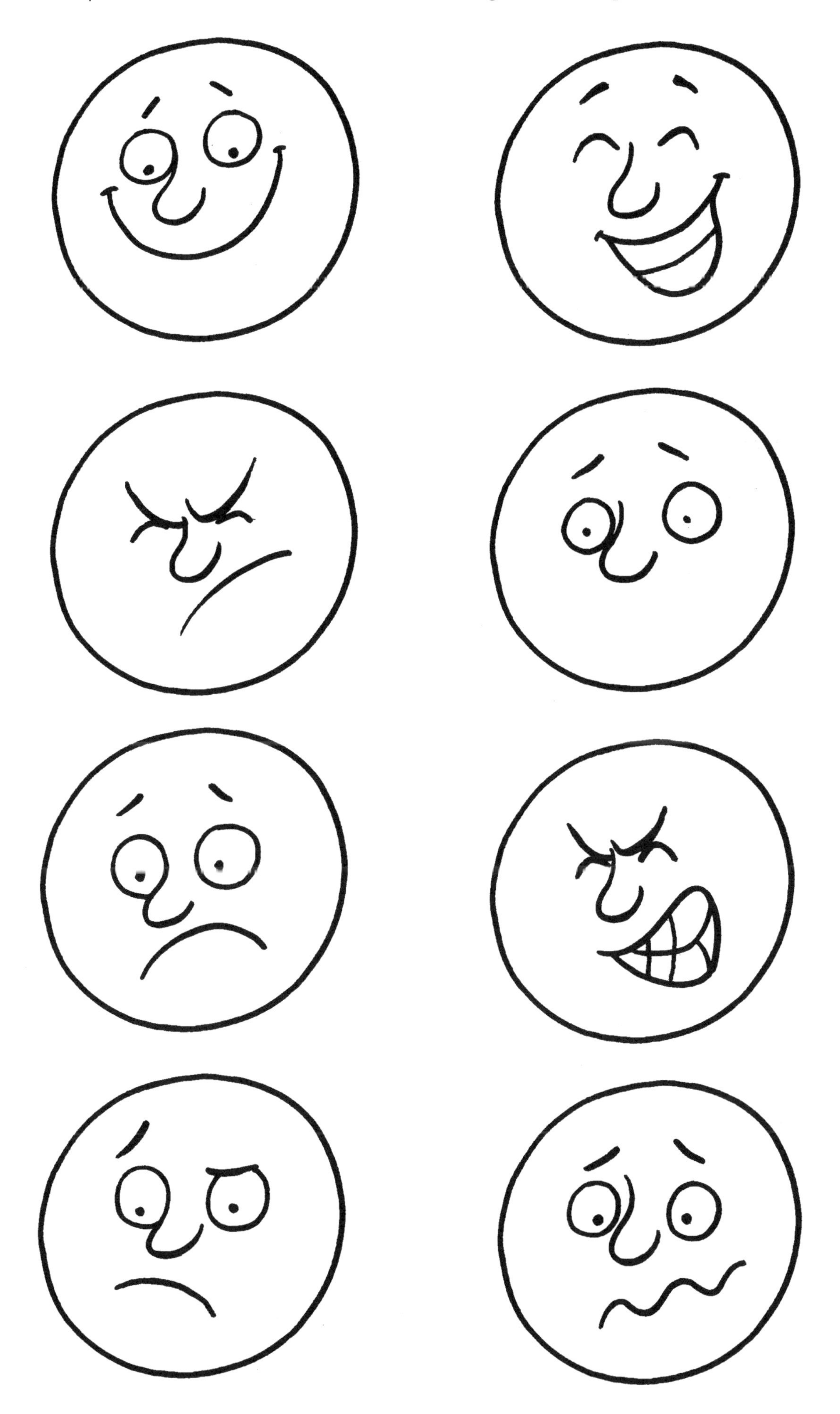

Drinks recipes for use with **Which is the best?**

Have fun making these delicious drinks

Which do you think is best? Why?

As you enjoy your drinks together talk about how Jesus can give us the very best too.

Coke float

Put a scoop of ice cream into a glass of coke. Decorate with hundreds and thousands.

Lemon and lime zapper

Mix lime juice and lemonade in a glass. Float lemon slices and ice cubes on top.

Taste of the tropics

Put two spoonfuls of tinned fruit salad in a glass. Top up with a mixture of any fruit juices you have available.

Glowing sunset

Mix orange juice and lemonade in a glass. Carefully pour in a little blackcurrant juice down the side of the glass. Admire the sunset effect.

If you make these drinks at home, remember to have an adult with you.

CORE PROGRAMME CONTINUED

wants to give the very best to everyone – to be friends with God. Encourage the children to look quietly at the sheet and tell Jesus what they think about him. You could finish by quietly playing the song 'God is an awesome God' from the *Light for Everyone* CD.

Balloon praise

⑤ - ⑩ ***minutes***

Why: to praise Jesus for giving us the best
With: inflated balloons, marker pens with ink that does not smudge, music (optional)

1 Inflate the balloons before the session and keep them in a pillowcase or bin liner to stop them escaping!

2 Challenge the children to think of words they would use to celebrate something (for example, 'hurray' or 'hallelujah'). Write down their suggestions for reference.

3 Give each child a balloon and a felt-tip pen and encourage them to write one of the words on the balloon (carefully!).

4 Encourage each child to bat their balloon to another child. When each has caught a balloon, shout out, 'Jesus gives the very best!' and then the children can respond with what is on their balloon.

5 Enjoy this for as many times as you like!

Game

⑩ ***minutes***

Why: to realise that Jesus is with us all the time

1 Remind the children that one way that Jesus gives us the best is by being with us all the time, no matter what we're doing.

2 Invite the children to think of an activity they like doing. When they've had enough time to think about it, ask them individually: '[*Name*], what do you like doing with your friend, Jesus?'

3 Challenge the children to mime their activity for the others to guess.

4 Once someone has guessed, encourage the children to copy the action all together before the next child has a turn.

Which is the best?

⑩ - ⑮ ***minutes***

Why: to think what we mean by 'the best'
With: recipes for drinks from page 56, ingredients, jugs, cups

1 Choose two or more drinks from the simple recipes on page 56 and invite the children to make them. (Supervise this carefully.)

2 Ask the children to try each drink and decide which is their favourite and why (remembering any allergy and dietary issues).

3 Discuss how they decided which drink was the 'best' – was this done on taste alone or colour, or did they consider whether it was healthy?

4 Explain that, in today's Bible story, Jesus made the very best drink out of something very ordinary.

Bubble writing for use with **Confetti picture**

JESUS GIVES THE BEST

EXTENSION IDEAS

Activities for younger children

Confetti picture

Why: to help the children realise that Jesus wants the best
With: boxes of confetti or scraps of coloured paper, bubble writing for posters from page 58 (optional)

1 Encourage the children to each write 'Jesus gives the best' on a sheet of paper (younger ones may need help) or give out copies of page 58 (enlarged, for a group poster).

2 Help them to decorate the paper with confetti, perhaps as a border or inside the bubble writing.

3 Encourage the children to stick their pictures up at home as a reminder that Jesus gives the best by helping us to be friends with God. Alternatively, as a group, make a poster-sized picture using confetti to fill in the bubble writing and display it in church.

Bible story picture

Why: to see how Jesus cared for people at a wedding party and helped them
With: a copy of the Bible story picture from page 60 (printed on A4 paper) for each child, a pot of water, red paint powder or food colouring, paint and brushes, cover-up and clean-up facilities

1 Use the picture to talk about Jesus and Mary at a wedding party. Ask the children to point out Jesus, Mary, the bride and the groom. Say Mary noticed that the wine was finished and told Jesus. Why do they think she told him? (*He cared about his friends and would know what to do to help them.*)

2 Say that Jesus told the servants to fill the big stone jars with water. Invite the children to dip their brushes into the water and 'paint' the water jars in their pictures with water.

3 What did Jesus do to the water? He changed it into wine to help his friends! Add red paint or food colouring to the water. Let the children use it to paint the jars again, to show the water turned to wine.

4 Encourage the children to complete their pictures. As they work, chat to them about how Jesus also cares for us and helps us.

For older children

Wedding gifts

Why: to help the children know that Jesus offers the very best
With: a selection of small boxes, wrapping paper and gift tags, or tags from page 61

1 Before the session, label the gift tags: 'To ...., Jesus gives you the very best.'

2 Explain that people take presents to a wedding, and Jesus wants to give us a present – the best kind of life with him.

3 Invite the children to choose a box and wrapping paper, and to wrap the box as if it was a present.

4 Give each child a gift tag and invite them to write their name on it and attach it to their 'gift'.

5 Encourage the children to put their 'gift' somewhere at home where they will see it, and to think about whether they want to respond to Jesus' offer of giving them the very best.

THE LEARN AND REMEMBER VERSE

'Jesus said, "I am the way, the truth and the life; no one goes to the Father except by me."'

John 14:6

Encourage your group to make up actions to each of the separate phrases so that they can teach the verse to someone else, who can teach it to someone else, who can… and so on. Challenge them to see how many people can learn it by next week.

Find a poster for this Learn and remember verse on page 79.

You could also use the song 'The way', on the *Bitesize Bible Songs 1* and *2* CDs (original version and a remix), available from Scripture Union.

Use with **Bible story picture**
Jesus helps John 2:1–11

Tag templates for use with **Wedding gifts**

Congratulations

To ....

Jesus gives you the very best

SERIES 3 JESUS SHOWS GOD'S LOVE

SESSION 2

Bread for life

Bible:
John 6:1–15,22–40

Aim: To be encouraged that Jesus knows and meets our needs

CORE PROGRAMME

For 3 to 14s

Bible story with movement

(20) *minutes*

Why: to be encouraged that Jesus knows and meets our needs
With: SU *Bible Timeline* or the *Big Bible Storybook Timeline* (optional; see page 96 for details)

1 **Background**
Show the children Moses on the SU *Bible Timeline* ('God frees his people') and explain that God had a plan for Moses and his people. Each day he gave them special bread called manna so that they would not be hungry. Invite the children to find 'Jesus teaches and heals' on the *Timeline*, and tell them that when a large crowd came to hear Jesus teach he gave them bread when they were hungry.

2 **Story**
Encourage your group to imagine they are part of the story as you tell it. (If you are short of space, this can be done without movement.)

Story: You live near Lake Galilee. *(Ask the children to tell what they can see from their house.)* It's a lovely day and you've heard that a special person, called Jesus, is nearby. Lots of your friends and their families are going to see him. You take a picnic. Let's see what's in your picnic basket. *(Pretend to open a box.)* You have five little rolls and two fish. After Mum gives you your lunch, off you go with your friends.

(All stand up and start to walk slowly around the room.) Which of your friends are there? *(Ask for suggestions.)* Lots and lots more people join in until there's a large crowd around the lake. *(Wave to other friends.)* Imagine a football field full of people. Now imagine ten football fields full of people. Imagine there are more than 5,000 people – maybe even 10,000!

All these people are talking about Jesus. What are you feeling now? *(Ask for suggestions.)* You then start climbing a grassy hill. Look! You can see Jesus and his special friends already up the hill. Everyone climbs the hill towards them. *(Act this out, wiping the sweat off your brows as you go.)* There's a big crowd, but you manage to get close to Jesus. Jesus is talking. Everyone is silent, listening to what he has to say. *(All stand still, listening to Jesus.)* You hear him say, 'I am the bread of life. Just as you must eat to live, you need me to give you all you need to help you live with God.'

Then you hear Jesus say to Philip, one of his friends: 'Where can we buy enough food to feed all these people?' You realise your tummy is rumbling too. *(Rub your tummy.)* Jesus seems to know everyone is hungry. Philip answers Jesus that it would cost a lot of money to give everyone some bread and they don't have that much money.

Another friend of Jesus, Andrew, comes up to you and asks what's in your picnic. You show him your five little loaves and two fish. With that, Andrew goes over to Jesus and tells him about your picnic. Jesus asks for it! What do you think he's going to do? Then you remember a story you heard about a big crowd of people who were hungry. A long time ago they were in the desert with no food. That story says how God knew that Moses and the people were hungry so he gave them special bread called manna. Might Jesus be able to do a miracle like that?

Jesus' friends tell everyone to sit down in groups. *(Do so.)* Then Jesus thanks God for your picnic and his friends start sharing it among the crowd. Wow! Everyone is getting enough bread to eat, even though you only gave him five little rolls!

Then Jesus does the same with the fish. Even more amazing, when everyone has had enough food to eat, the friends of Jesus gather up the leftovers!

What might you say to Jesus right now?

3 **Pray**
Turn the children's suggestions into a prayer.

Chat

 - (10) ***minutes***

Why: to understand the concept of needs

1 Explain that a 'need' is something you can't live without, but a 'want' is something that may make you happy but you can live without.

2 Give each child a sheet of paper and a pencil. Ask them to draw something they have that they need, and something they want to keep, but could do without if they had to.

3 Invite everyone to describe what they have drawn, explaining why one is needed and one is just a luxury.

4 Use the ideas as a focus for prayer. Thank God for all that he has given us!

Model making

 ***minutes***

Why: to understand some of our needs
With: plastic bricks, instructions for making a dog-shape below (optional)

1 Ask the children what we need to live, for example, food and fresh air. Help the group work out the difference between what we want and what we need.

2 Give the children instructions for making a model. Challenge them to work out what they need to make the model. Give out the model pieces as they ask for them.

3 Say that today's Bible story is about some people who needed something. Jesus gave them what they needed immediately, but also offered them much more.

Write and thank

 ***minutes***

Why: to remember that Jesus meets all our needs, not just those for food

1 Ask the children what needs they have. If you did 'Model making', review the list of 'needs' the children came up with. If not, make a list now. Make a table with two columns, labelled 'Body needs – things we can touch' and 'Heart needs – things we need even more'. Encourage the children to work out which ideas from their list go in which column.

2 Invite the children to take it in turns to choose one of the needs they would like to thank God for meeting. See if any of the children would like to say thanks personally and encourage them to pray.

PHOTOCOPIABLE PART

Diagram for use with **Model making**

How to make your own model dog from plastic bricks

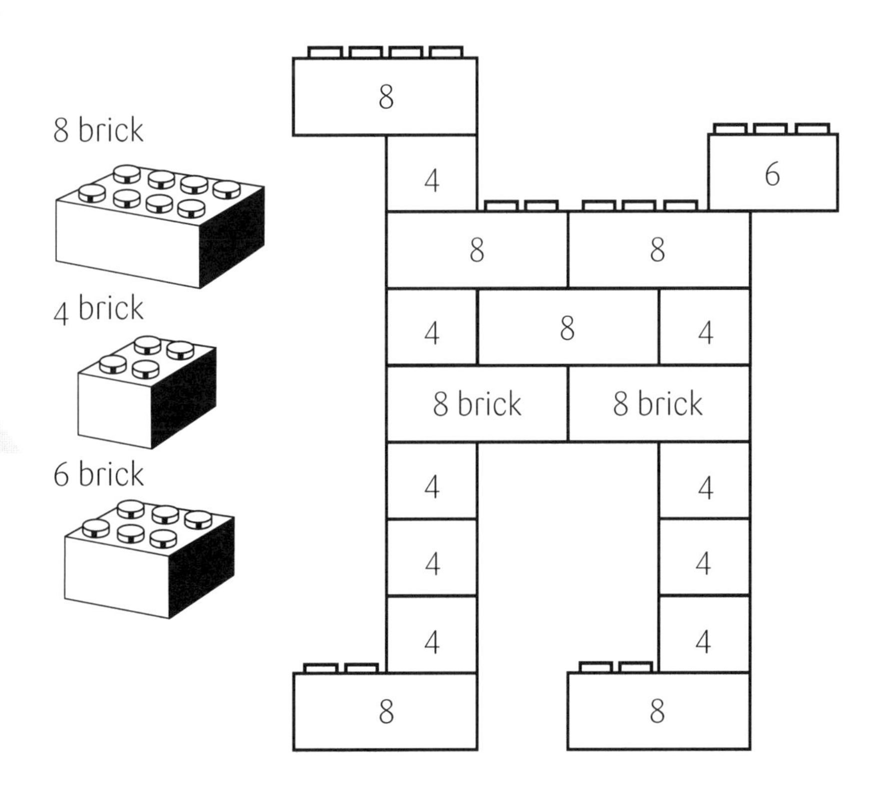

EXTENSION IDEAS

Activities for younger children

Draw a picture

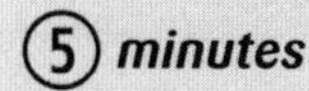

Why: to pray to Jesus, who can provide for our needs
With: paper, crayons

1 Talk to the children about what the people in the Bible story needed. Why did they need food? Who helped them? What did he do?

2 Say that Jesus can still help us and provide us with what we need. Ask the children to think of some things they need, such as food, clothes, water, homes and families. Suggest they draw a picture of some of these things. Give out the paper and crayons and chat to the children about what they are drawing.

3 When they have finished, spread out the pictures so everyone can see them, while you pray together. Say, 'Thank you, Jesus, that you provided food for hungry people. Thank you that you can provide us with what we need. Thank you for giving us... *(name the things in the pictures)*.

Bible story picture

Why: to see how Jesus provided what was needed most
With: *The Big Bible Storybook* (hardback or audio), a copy of the Bible story picture from page 65 (printed on A4 paper) for each child, gummed coloured paper (pre-cut into fish shapes for younger children; two per child), scissors, crayons

1 Read 'Bread for everyone' from *The Big Bible Storybook* page 165, or tell the Bible story in your own words.

2 Hand out the pictures. Talk about the crowds of people who followed Jesus. Encourage the children to discuss how the people felt after the long journey (*tired and hungry*). Jesus knew they needed food. There was no money to buy food, but Jesus knew what to do. Ask the children to show you Jesus. Who do they see standing next to Jesus? What does he have with him? What did Jesus say to the crowds? What happened then? Did everyone have enough to eat?

3 Ask the children what is missing from the picture (*the fish*). Ask them to draw two fish each, cut them out and stick them on the picture (use pre-cut shapes for younger children). The pictures can also be coloured in, if time permits. As everyone works, chat about how Jesus also knows exactly what we need and provides for us.

For older children

What we need

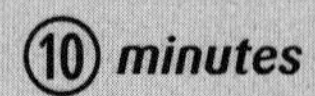

Why: to understand how God provides for our spiritual needs
With: copies of page 66, scissors, a plate or shallow bowl, music

1 Read out what Jesus said in John 6:35.

2 Challenge the children to think of ways in which Jesus 'feeds' us. Ask: 'What does he give us that we need?' and 'Why does he give us these things?'

3 Give each child a copy of page 66. Encourage them to write their ideas on the shapes, cut them out and put them on a plate.

4 Invite the children to sit in a circle. Play some music and pass the plate round the group.

5 When the music stops, invite the person holding the plate to choose a shape and pray, 'Lord Jesus, please give us all... to help us...' (using the words on the shapes).

THE LEARN AND REMEMBER VERSE

'Jesus said, "I am the way, the truth, and the life; no one goes to the Father except by me."'

John 14:6

Say the verse a few times, facing north, east, south and west for each phrase. Challenge the children to tell how this verse relates to today's Bible story.

Find a poster for this Learn and remember verse on page 79.

You could also use the song 'The way', on the *Bitesize Bible Songs 1* and *2* CDs (original version and a remix), available from Scripture Union.

Use with **Bible story picture**
Jesus feeds John 6:1–15

Bread and fish for use with **What we need**

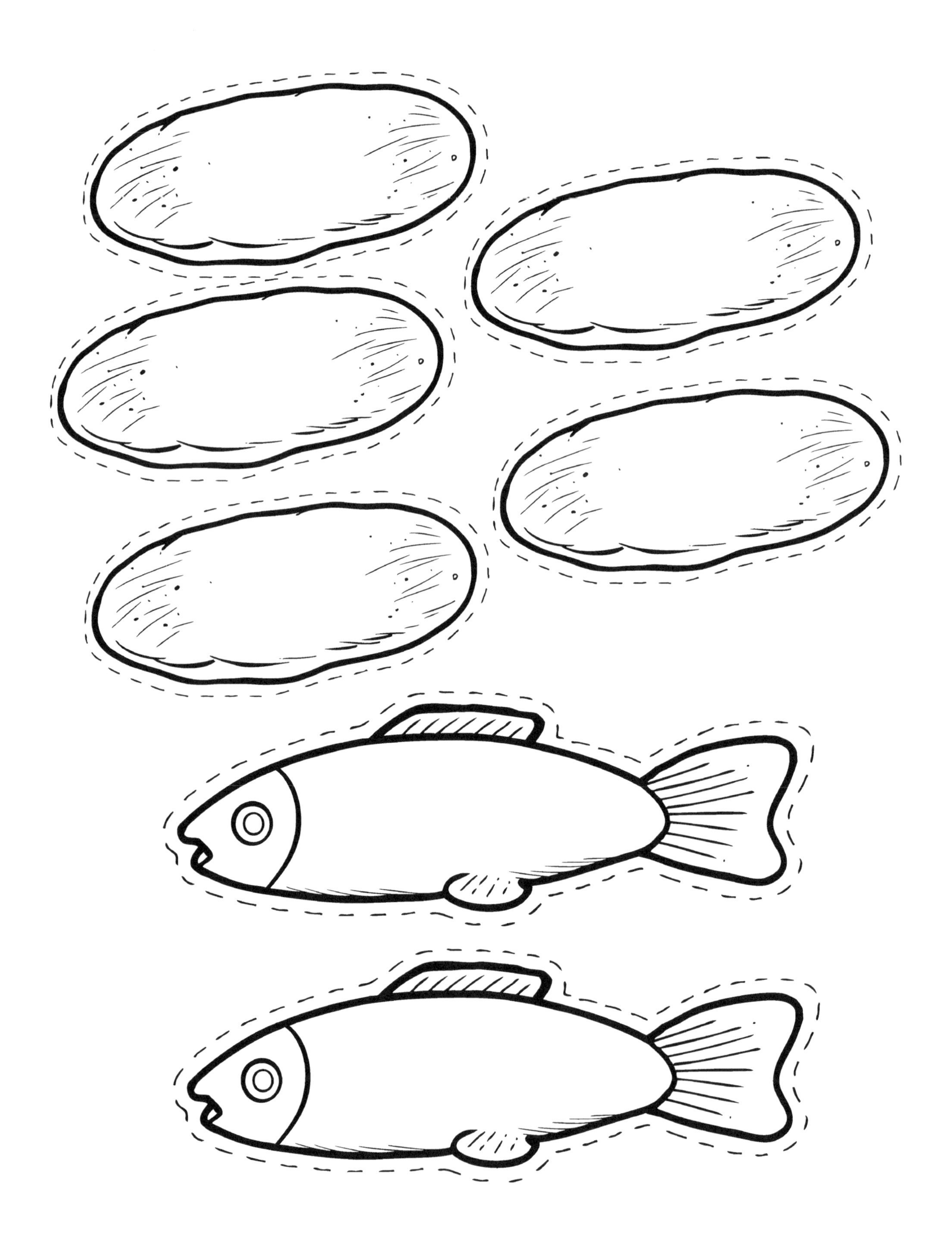

SESSION 3

Good shepherd

Bible:
John 10:1–15

Aim: To realise that Jesus loves and protects his people

CORE PROGRAMME

For 3 to 14s

Shepherd mime

(10) - (15) ***minutes***

Why: to realise that Jesus loves and protects his people
With: SU *Bible Timeline* or the *Big Bible Storybook Timeline* (see page 96 for details)

1 ***Bible Timeline***
Challenge the children to find anyone mentioned on the *Timeline* who was a shepherd (for example, Jacob, Joseph, Moses and David). Ask: 'What about Jesus?' Look together at the picture of the crucifixion. Say that today they will find out why Jesus said he was like a good shepherd.

2 **Action story**
Invite the children to work in threes. They are going to act the parts of a good shepherd, a bad shepherd and a sheep. (There can be more than one sheep in each group if necessary.)

Read the following script, pausing at the ✱ to allow the children time to pose or make appropriate sounds.

Story: Let me introduce you to my sheep ✱. Let's call her Sheila. Sheila can bleat loudly ✱. When Sheila gets scared she bleats REALLY loudly ✱. Sheila is looked after by a good shepherd ✱ and a bad shepherd ✱ who both work for me.

The good shepherd smiles at Sheila ✱. He loves her to bits. It's getting late so it's time to take Sheila to her sheep pen ✱. The shepherd leads the way, and walks round the sheep pen to check there are no holes in the wall that Sheila could escape from. He opens the gate, leads Sheila inside and closes the gate, waving goodbye as he leaves ✱.

The next day is the bad shepherd's turn to look after Sheila. The bad shepherd didn't like getting up early to go to work so he scowls at Sheila ✱. It's time to go to the nearby field. Sheila starts eating the pathetic few blades of grass. The bad shepherd lies down to have a sleep ✱. Oh no! There's a wolf coming! Sheila runs back to the pen, bleating loudly ✱. The bad shepherd runs away. Fortunately, the wolf was full already! Before the end of his turn, the bad shepherd sneaks off home without saying goodbye to Sheila ✱.

The following morning the good shepherd is back. The shepherd opens the gate. He calls his sheep by name ✱. Sheila recognises the good shepherd's voice and is pleased to see him ✱. Sheila would not have come to the call of the bad shepherd. She's much too smart! The good shepherd leads his sheep to a nearby field. When they get there Sheila starts eating the gorgeous green grass. The good shepherd looks out for danger ✱. Oh no! There's a wolf coming! The good shepherd fights the wolf, swings him round and round and throws him far, far away ✱. What a brave shepherd! That was a close shave for him and Sheila! He could have been killed. But the shepherd and sheep are still alive and Sheila bleats a thank-you 'baa' ✱

3 **Respond**
Choose a volunteer to read John 10:10–15. Encourage the group to notice that Jesus knows his sheep and they know him. Ask the children who they think the sheep are and what the good shepherd in the story did that risked his life. (*He fought the wolf.*) Say that, like a good shepherd, Jesus knows every one of us by name and was willing to die so that we could be forgiven and be loved by God for ever. Invite the children to think about Jesus as their good shepherd. Ask: 'What would you like to say to him now?'

CORE PROGRAMME CONTINUED

Plaster praise

(10) - (15) ***minutes***

Why: to think about God's protection
With: large washable sticking plasters, a large doll or the person outline below

1 Give each child a pen and a sticking plaster. (Be aware of allergies; you could use small strips of paper and strips of sticky tape instead.)

2 Encourage the children to think of ways in which God protects them day by day, and to write them on the plasters. Invite them to share what they have written.

3 Stick the plasters on the doll or on the body parts of the picture where you might expect to have a plaster: elbows, fingers, legs and knees.

4 Holding the figure, use their ideas in a prayer for God's protection every day.

Sheepfold

(5) - (10) ***minutes***

Why: to think about Jesus as the Good Shepherd

1 Encourage the children to form a circle, linking arms but leaving a space between two of them.

2 Stand in the centre of the circle and explain that you are the sheep and they are the fold, and that the space is the gate.

3 Look scared and say that there is a wolf coming. What could they do? (*Hopefully, close up the gap!*)

4 Say a prayer, thanking God for helping us in times of danger.

5 Look pleased and say that the shepherd is coming. What should they do? (*Hopefully, open the gate!*)

6 Go out of the gate saying that you're following the shepherd to nice grass! Thank Jesus for giving you good things.

7 Repeat, inviting different children to be sheep and thinking of different things to give thanks for.

Protection

(5) ***minutes***

Why: to think about how things protect us
With: pictures from page 69

1 Look with the children at the selection of items on page 69, but keep the shepherd's crook picture covered. Challenge the children to think of ways in which these items keep us safe. (You could give them individual pictures to comment on.)

2 Uncover the picture of the shepherd's crook. Ask: 'What is it? Who uses it? What is it for?' Challenge the children to think how it could have something to do with their protection. Explain that today they will find out that Jesus described himself as a shepherd.

PHOTOCOPIABLE PART

Person outline
for use with
Plaster praise

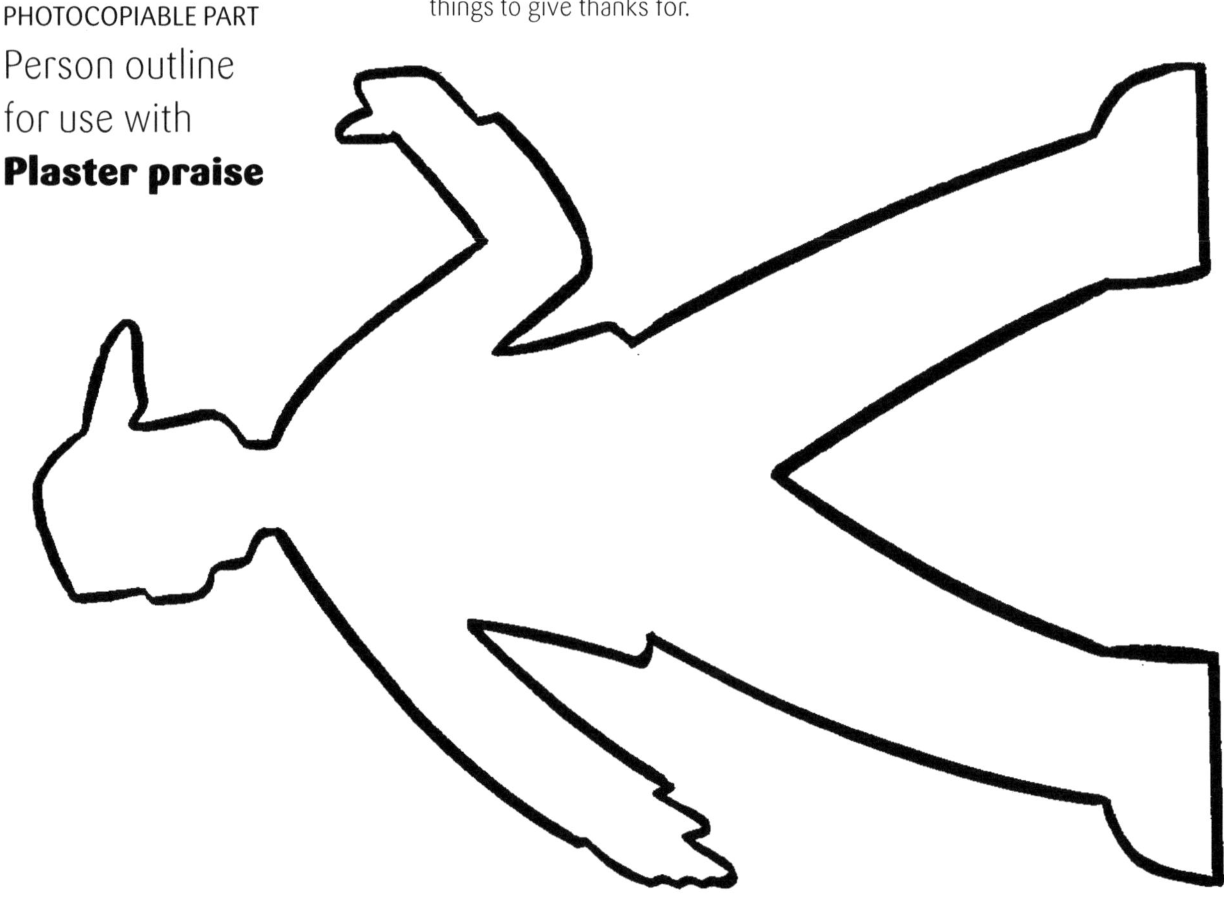

Pictures for use with **Protection**

EXTENSION IDEAS

Activities for younger children

Jesus knows me

5 - 10 *minutes*

Why: to appreciate that Jesus knows and loves us
With: A4 card, sheep templates from page 71 (optional)

1 Invite the children to make a sheep-shaped card. Help them to fold their card in half, draw a sheep on it, with its back touching the fold, and cut it out (a template is available on page 71).

2 Encourage them to write their name on the front of the sheep and put some facts about themselves inside. Assure them that no one else will read the card, so they can write whatever they want.

3 Invite them to hold their card as you read John 10:3 and 14, reminding them that Jesus knows everything about them.

4 Invite them to write verse 11 around the edge of their sheep and to put it somewhere at home to remind them of how much Jesus loves them.

Bible story picture

8 - 10 *minutes*

Why: to feel God's love and protection
With: a copy of the picture from page 72 (printed on A4 paper) for each child, one enlarged copy, crayons

1 Show the enlarged picture and briefly tell the Bible story. Ask the children where the shepherd is. What is he doing? Why is he sleeping in the gateway instead of in a bed? How do they think the sheep feel? Can they get lost? Can a robber steal them? Can a wolf get to them? Chat about how the shepherd loves and protects his sheep.

2 Hand out the pictures and pretend they are stones. Arrange them in a circle to make a sheep pen, leaving a gap for the gate. Take turns to be the shepherd on guard while everyone else in the group has fun being sheep safe inside the pen.

3 When it is your turn to be the shepherd, encourage the 'sheep' to rest. Talk about how safe they feel.

4 Let the children enjoy colouring their pictures. As they work, chat about how God loves and protects us just as the shepherd does his sheep.

For older children

Picture puzzle

10 *minutes*

Why: to think about ways Jesus loves and protects us
With: copies of the picture from page 73

1 Give each child or pair of children a copy of page 73. See how many things and people they can identify that protect us.

2 Pause after they have found a few. Ask questions comparing their findings to Jesus, such as: 'How does Jesus protect us like a mother does?; How does Jesus protect us like a police officer does?'

3 See how many protective things and people they can find. Continue asking them questions and encouraging them to think about how Jesus protects us as they colour in all the things they have found.

THE LEARN AND REMEMBER VERSE

'Jesus said, "I am the way, the truth and the life; no one goes to the Father except by me."'

John 14:6

With: a large sheet of paper or card, glue, wool

Working together, encourage the children to write out the verse by gluing pieces of wool to a large sheet of paper. Display the woollen verses on the wall and learn it.

Find a poster for this Learn and remember verse on page 79.

You could also use the song 'The way', on the *Bitesize Bible Songs 1* and *2* CDs (original version and a remix), available from Scripture Union.

Sheep templates for use with **Jesus knows me**

Use with **Bible story picture**
Jesus protects John 10:1–15

Picture for use with **Picture puzzle**

SERIES 3 JESUS SHOWS GOD'S LOVE

SESSION 4

Death to life

Bible:
John 11:1–44

Aim: To believe that Jesus gives life

CORE PROGRAMME

For 3 to 14s

Bible story with responses

(20) *minutes*

Why: to believe that Jesus gives life
With: *Light for Everyone* CD and means to play it, SU *Bible Timeline* or the *Big Bible Storybook Timeline* (see page 96 for details) (all optional)

1 ***Bible Timeline***
Challenge the children to find as many pictures of Jesus as they can on the SU *Bible Timeline*. Say that today they will hear a story about a time when Jesus wasn't where some of his friends wanted him to be.

2 **Prepare**
Write an 'E' for 'Everyone' on one sheet of paper and a 'J' for 'Jesus' on a second sheet.

Tell the children that you need their help in today's story. When you hold up the 'E', they must say Jesus' words: **'Everyone who believes in me will live, even though they die.'** When you hold up the 'J', they should use Jesus' friends' words: **'Jesus, where were you?'** (These are shown in bold in the text below.) If the children want to, they could make up an action to go with each phrase; write the phrases on the sheets, if necessary. Practise together before you start the story.

3 **Story**
Jesus had a friend called Lazarus, who lived in Bethany. He was very ill. His sisters, Mary and Martha, sent Jesus a message, to ask him to help Lazarus.

Then Jesus said, **'Everyone who believes in me will live, even though they die.'**

But Jesus stayed where he was for two more days. By now, Lazarus had died. Jesus told his disciples, 'Lazarus is dead. Now you will have a chance to believe in me. Let's go to him.' They remembered that Jesus said, **'Everyone who believes in me will live, even though they die.'**

When they got to Bethany, Lazarus' sister Martha said, **'Jesus, where were you?'** She continued, 'If you had been here my brother would not have died.'

The disciples remembered that Jesus said, **'Everyone who believes in me will live, even though they die.'** Jesus told Martha, 'Your brother will live again.'

Martha replied, 'I know one day he will live again.'

Jesus told Martha, 'I am the one who raises the dead to life!' Then he told her, **'Everyone who believes in me will live, even though they die.'** Jesus asked Martha, 'Do you believe this?'

'Yes,' said Martha.

Then she went to see her sister Mary. 'Jesus is here. He wants to see you,' she told her.

When Mary met Jesus, she asked him, **'Jesus, where were you?'** She continued, 'If you had been here my brother would not have died.'

Jesus said, 'Where have you put his body?'

Mary took Jesus to the tomb. It was a cave with a stone rolled over the door. Lots of Lazarus' friends were there. They were all very sad. When Jesus saw the tomb he was very sad too.

The friends said, 'Jesus, where were you?' They continued, 'If you can make blind people see, why couldn't you keep Lazarus from dying?'

The disciples were beginning to wonder what Jesus meant when he said, **'Everyone who believes in me will live, even though they die.'**

Jesus got them to roll the stone away. Jesus prayed. Then he shouted, 'Lazarus, come out!' Lazarus came out alive! His hands and feet were wrapped with strips of cloth and there was a cloth over his face. Jesus asked Mary and Martha to untie him.

4 **Respond**
Hold up the first sheet of paper again for the children to say the phrase, **'Everyone who believes in me will live, even though they die.'** Explain that Jesus gives people who love him the best kind of life because he is there to help them follow his way. It also means that when our bodies die the person that is 'you' carries on living with God for ever. Jesus wanted this for everyone, not just Lazarus.

Allow the children time to respond to this. (They may have a lot of questions about death; be sensitive to anything they might want to say.) Then sing together a song such as 'God is an awesome God' from the *Light for Everyone* CD.

Life rap

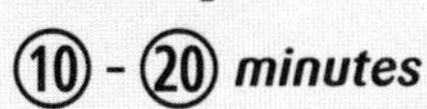 ***minutes***

Why: to remember that Jesus gives life
With: percussion instruments (optional), words for the rap below

1 Working in pairs or all together, encourage the children to make up a dance sequence that can be performed while saying the rap below. Encourage them to use the instruments provided or anything suitable in your meeting room.

2 Perform the rap together, stressing the syllables marked in bold type.

Life game

 ***minutes***

Why: to rejoice that Jesus gives life
With: *Reach Up!* CD and means to play it (optional)

1 Encourage the children to think of ways that show they have life (for example, they can move and breathe and grow).

2 Help them create a movement for each thing they think of (for example, stand still and breathe slowly; reach up tall; move around). Invite them to think of an action for 'Jesus gives life'.

3 Call out the ideas at random, challenging the children to do the appropriate action as quickly as possible.

4 Finish with 'Jesus gives life' and give a shout of praise, or sing a song such as 'King of all' from the *Reach Up!* CD.

Poster painting

 ***minutes***

Why: to celebrate that Jesus gives life
With: paints, brushes, a long roll of paper, newspapers

1 Cover the floor or a long table with newspapers (for protection) and spread out the roll of paper. Invite the children to suggest colours that make them think of life. As they suggest a colour, encourage a chant of: 'Thank you, Jesus, for orange. Thank you, Jesus, for life.'

2 Invite them to paint one colour of their choice on the paper in any way they choose (or decide together how you will decorate it).

3 When the paper is full of colour, paint 'Jesus gives life' in a contrasting colour over the top.

4 Together, praise Jesus for giving us life.

PHOTOCOPIABLE PART

Words for use with

Life rap

Jesus has the **power** over **life** and **death**.
Life and **death**! **Life** and **death**!
His **friend** called **Laz**arus **sad**ly **died**.
Life and **death**! **Life** and **death**!
Not for **long**, Jesus brought him **back** to **life**.
Life and **death**! **Life** and **death**!
Everyone **there** was **ve**ry sur**prised**.
Life and **death**! **Life** and **death**!
Now that they had **seen** it with their **ve**ry own **eyes**.
Life and **death**! **Life** and **death**!
They **should** have known 'It's **not** the **end**' when Jesus **died**.
Life and **death**! **Life** and **death**!
But **first** they had to **see** him, then they **star**ted to get **wise**.
Life and **death**! **Life** and **death**!
Faith in **Je**sus **means** that **we'll** have
Life and **life** and **life** and **life**!

Template for use with **Lazarus model**

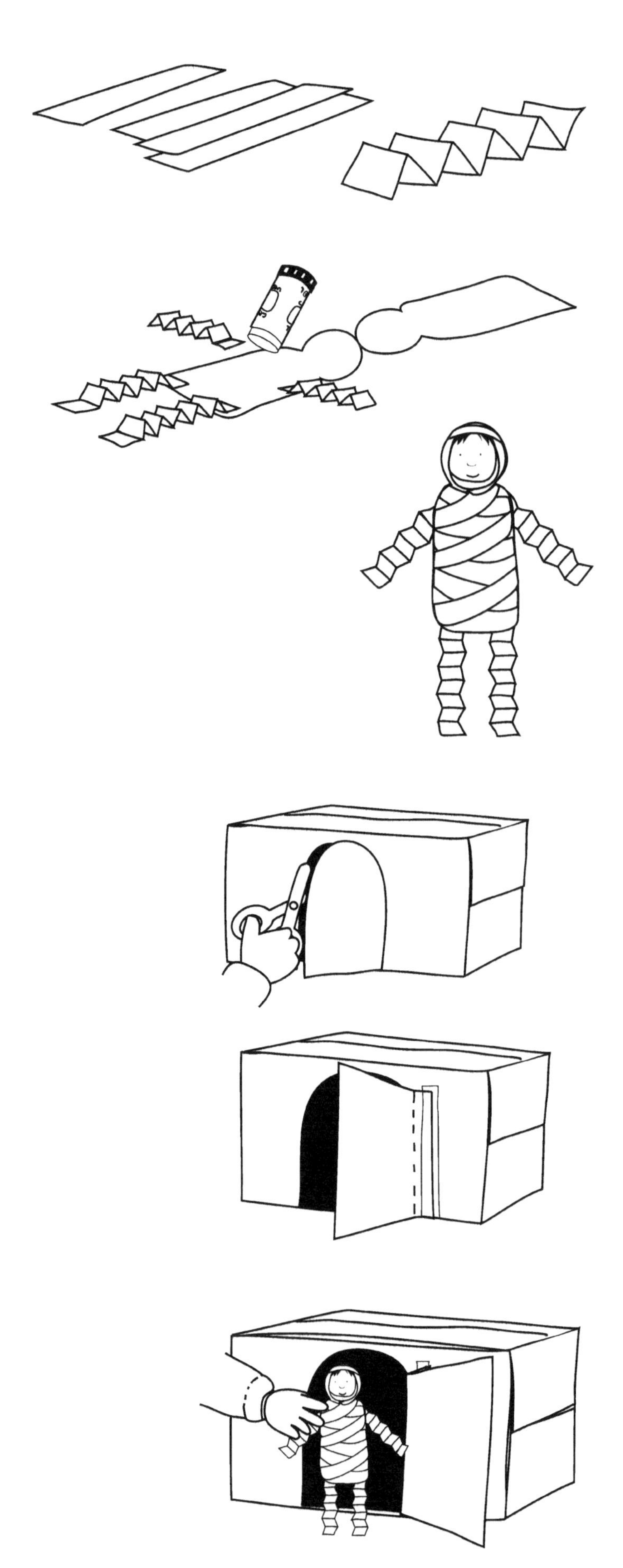

EXTENSION IDEAS

Activities for younger children

Lazarus model

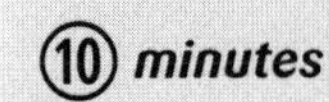

Why: to visualise Jesus giving Lazarus life
With: Lazarus model from page 76, narrow strips of paper, large plastic bottles or boxes, sticky tape, glue sticks, art materials, cover-up and clean-up equipment

1 Prepare a Lazarus model beforehand as an example (see page 76). Place Lazarus in the cave (made from a bottle or box, and decorated if you have time). Talk about how Lazarus was put into a cave after he died. Peep inside your cave and see him lying still. Explain that everyone was very sad and cried, but then Jesus did something amazing. He called, 'Lazarus, come out,' and Lazarus walked out! Open the cave flap, take Lazarus out and jiggle him around so his arms and legs wiggle about. Say that Jesus had given him his life back.

2 Help the children to make their own models of Lazarus and the cave. Encourage them to use their models to tell how Jesus brought Lazarus back to life, something that ordinary people cannot do.

3 Suggest that the children use the models to tell the Bible story to their families.

Bible story picture

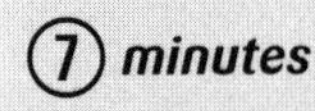

Why: to see that Jesus can do something that an ordinary person cannot do
With: a copy of the picture from page 78 (printed on A4 paper) for each child with an A4 sheet of blank paper fixed to the picture along the top edge, crayons

1 Hand out the papers, so the children are looking at the blank top sheet.

2 Talk about how Martha and Mary were sad and cried when their brother, Lazarus, died. Jesus was also very sad and went to see them. He told Martha that Lazarus would live again. They all went to the cave in which Lazarus' body had been put. Jesus talked to God and then called, 'Lazarus! Come out!'

3 Suggest the children lift up the flaps on their pictures to see what happened next. Who can they see? Are the people happy or sad? Did Lazarus get up and come out of the cave? Help the children realise that Lazarus was alive again – Jesus had done something no ordinary person could do and had brought him back to life.

4 Ask the children to draw a picture on the flap of Jesus calling to Lazarus.

5 Encourage them to use their pictures to tell the Bible story to each other, lifting the flap at the moment when something amazing happens!

For older children

Praying with water

(10) *minutes*

Why: praying for those who are suffering
With: a bottle with a small hole in the cap filled with lightly salted water, a glass bowl

1 Shake a few drops of water into the bowl from the bottle and ask whether it reminds the group of anything – perhaps rain or tears. Taste it and assure the group that it's saltwater – like tears.

2 Ask the young people to pass the bottle round. As they each hold the bottle, ask them to think of a situation in the world or in their own life that might be making Jesus weep. They can then bring that situation to God and shake a few drops of water into the bowl as a sign that they know God shares in the suffering.

3 Finish by reading one or more of these verses:

'You have recorded my troubles. You have kept a list of my tears.' (Psalm 56:8)

'[The Lord said,] I have heard your prayer and seen your tears, so I will heal you.' (2 Kings 20:5)

'[God] will wipe away every tear from their eyes.' (Revelation 21:4)

THE LEARN AND REMEMBER VERSE

'Jesus said, "I am the way, the truth and the life; no one goes to the Father except by me."'

John 14:6

Challenge the children to design a maze on a large sheet of paper that takes them past the words of the verse in the right order. Remind them to leave two gaps in the maze – to enter and leave by.

Find a poster for this Learn and remember verse on page 79.

You could also use the song 'The way', on the *Bitesize Bible Songs 1* and *2* CDs (original version and a remix), available from Scripture Union.

Use with **Bible story picture**
Jesus gives life John 11:17–44

'Jesus said, "I am the way, the truth and the life; no one goes to the Father except by me."

John 14:6

SERIES 4

SERIES INTRODUCTION

DARING DANIEL

Daniel shows the uniqueness of God. God's desire to rescue his people is illustrated in the life of Daniel

BIBLE BACKGROUND FOR YOU

In 587 BC Jerusalem fell to the Babylonians and many of its inhabitants were taken into exile. This was the normal practice of victorious powers in the ancient world - it ensured that the conquered people were weakened and less able to rebel. For the Jewish people this was a deeply painful and confusing experience, raising questions about their identity and their faith.

Daniel was one of the first to be taken to Babylon - probably before the final fall of Jerusalem. In Babylon he quickly made a mark for himself. His faith in God shone through despite the confusion of being in exile as he refused to compromise his principles or his devotion to God.

Like Daniel, we live in a world that is constantly pressuring us to conform to its patterns. How far do we trust God to see us through difficult times? To what extent are we prepared to stand out against the pressure of society? The children in our groups see us as role models. The way we live communicates as powerfully to them as the things that we say.

For your small group with a wide age range

Increasingly our children are growing up in a culture that does not acknowledge God. It was the same for Daniel and his friends, the characters in this series. They worked out how to be different as Jews in Babylon; they trusted in God's protection in the alien culture.

Our children may find themselves challenged to be different in today's world and discover they can turn to God in difficult situations. For the youngest ones, for whom such challenges are not appropriate, it is enough that they are offered concrete examples of doing what's right and trusting God.

Resources for ministry

Daniel

For the youngest children in your group, this retelling of the story of Daniel comes as a chunky board book, with 24 pages so it has the sense of being a 'real' book with lots of pages. Especially for under-5s, it features full-colour photographic spreads of the much-loved *Bible Friends* characters from *The Big Bible Storybook*. It is perfectly sized for small hands, with short text for a parent, leader or carer to read to the child.

£3.99

ISBN 978 1 84427 710 0

Highlights from *LightLive*

Go to the 'Search *LightLive*' tab at www.lightlive.org and enter this session's Bible reference to find:

- 'Audio Bible story': a regular mp3 download for 3–7s
- 'Learn and remember': a PowerPoint of a Bible verse to learn, for 5–11s (see also page 90)
- 'Presentation': an activity with animation for 11–14s

SERIES 4 DARING DANIEL

SESSION 1

Daniel is different

Bible:
Daniel 1

Aim: To discover that God's people should live differently

CORE PROGRAMME

For 3 to 14s

Bible story with food

(15) ***minutes***

Why: to discover that God's people should live differently
With: pieces of raw fruit and vegetables, sweets, crisps, chocolate, water, fizzy drinks (or use plastic vegetables, packets and bottles), cups, two trays, SU *Bible Timeline* or the *Big Bible Storybook Timeline* (see page 96 for details)

1 **SU *Bible Timeline***
Ask the children to look along the Old Testament part of the *Bible Timeline* and find the picture that shows when the people were ruled by kings. Explain that the people were pleased to have kings to rule over them but, unfortunately, most of the kings were bad and led the people to worship other gods. God sent them many warnings, but they didn't take any notice and this led to disaster. Ask someone to read the title of the next picture ('God punishes his people'). Explain that exile meant that they were living in a foreign country. Say that King Nebuchadnezzar had captured Jerusalem, taken the people prisoner and forced them to go and live in the city of Babylon.

2 **Acting the story**
Explain that King Nebuchadnezzar wanted some young men from Judah to be trained for three years to help run the country. Four of the men chosen were Daniel, Hananiah, Mishael and Azariah. *(Choose four children to play these roles and ask all the children to repeat their names after you. The rest of the children are to be the other young men.)*

Explain that the king ordered that all the young men should eat the same rich food and drink the same wine as he himself ate and drank. Put a tray with the rich food (sweets, crisps, chocolate) and fizzy drink in front of the children. Read Daniel 1:8–10. Explain that God had given his people strict rules about what they should eat so that they would stay healthy. Ask the children representing Daniel and his friends what they think they should do and why.

Read verses 11–14. Take a tray with pieces of raw vegetables and cups of water and place it in front of Daniel and his friends. Allow both groups to eat from their trays. (Be aware of hygiene and allergies.) While they are eating, ask the

children what they think will happen at the end of the ten days. Will Daniel and his friends look worse than the others? Will they get into trouble for disobeying the king?

After a little while, tell them that the ten days are up. Go and inspect each group. Ask them to stand up and do some exercises. Read verses 15 and 16. Say that all the young men were trained for three years. God made Daniel and his three friends clever and wise.

Choose a child to be the king and sit them on a throne. Say that the three years have now passed. Ask all the children to come and stand before the king. Read verses 18–20. Ask the king to choose Daniel, Hananiah, Mishael and Azariah and to send all the others away.

CORE PROGRAMME CONTINUED

3 **Think about**
Ask all the children to sit down and allow them to eat something from the other group's tray, if they wish. Explain that this story is not really about eating healthy food or eating only vegetables. Daniel and his friends chose to live differently from the other young men. Why? Because they knew that that was the way God wanted them to live. Explain that God still wants his people to live differently from other people. If possible, talk about a time when you had to choose to do something differently from those around you. Ask the children to close their eyes and, if they wish, tell God that they want to live his way.

Different worship

Why: to praise God, who helps us to live differently
With: psalm verses from page 83, worship music

1 Give out copies of Psalm 145:1–7 (page 83). Invite the children to underline different words for talking about God (for example: 'praise', 'mighty') as you read it out.

2 Encourage them to take it in turns to use these words to praise God for making their lives different in the past year, for example: 'Thank you, God, for healing Jake's knee.'

3 Say that one thing that is different (or distinctive) about Christians is that we praise God! Sing or listen to favourite worship songs chosen by the children.

Collage

Why: to think about living God's way
With: a large sheet of paper, photographs, magazines, newspapers

1 In advance, label a large sheet of paper 'God's way'. Select some age-appropriate pictures and newspaper headlines showing people from different ethnic groups doing 'good' and 'bad' things (check the reverse of your chosen items for inappropriate content!).

2 Explain that, like Daniel, we often have to choose to live differently from other people around us.

3 Invite the children to look through the pictures and headlines, deciding whether the people are living God's way or not. Encourage them each to choose some 'God's way' pictures and glue them to the paper to make a poster. Some children might like to draw their own ideas of people living God's way and stick them on to the poster.

Taste the difference

Why: to find out how we can live differently for God
With: three bowls, plain and flavoured crisps, plain ring-shaped crisps

1 Tip the plain crisps into the bowls. Pick up the first bowl and say that, mostly, people around us don't know God personally.

2 Say that God's people are different and he wants us to live differently. Show the flavoured crisps. Add them to the second bowl and say that sometimes there's no obvious difference!

3 Put four ring-shaped crisps into bowl three and ask if the children can spot the difference. Give at least one of these to each child to put on their fingers as they think about ways in which they can live differently for God.

4 Enjoy eating the crisps! (Be aware of allergy and hygiene issues.)

Psalm verses for use with **Different worship**

[1] **I will praise you, my God and King,**
and always honour your name.

[2] **I will praise you each day and always**
honour your name.

[3] **You are wonderful, LORD, and you deserve all praise,**
because you are much greater than anyone
can understand.

[4] **Each generation will announce to the next**
your wonderful and powerful deeds.

[5] **I will keep thinking about your marvellous glory**
and your mighty miracles.

[6] **Everyone will talk about your fearsome deeds,**
and I will tell all nations how great you are.

[7] **They will celebrate and sing**
about your matchless mercy and your power to save.

EXTENSION IDEAS

Activities for younger children

Enjoying vegetables

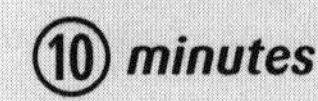
10 *minutes*

Why: to see that God will help us to choose what is right
With: small pieces of different vegetables suitable for children to eat, paper napkins

1 For this and any activity involving food, be aware of health, safety, hygiene and allergy issues.

2 Give each child a napkin and different vegetables. Encourage them to look carefully at the colours, patterns and textures of the vegetables. Give the children enough time to explore, ask questions and make comments. Let them eat the vegetables, if they wish.

3 Remind everyone that Daniel knew it was not right to eat the food the king gave him. What did he do? What did he ask to be given instead? He asked for vegetables, just like the ones the children have. He chose to eat what God wanted him to eat.

4 Ask the children whether they think it was hard for Daniel to choose to do the right thing. Help them to see that it was. Daniel needed God to help him.

5 Pray: 'Please, God, help us do the right thing, even when it's hard.'

Bible story picture

5 - 10 *minutes*

Why: to discover that God will help us choose what is right
With: a copy of the picture from page 85 (printed on A4 paper) for each child or enlarged copies for group use, art and craft materials, pictures of fruit and vegetables cut from magazines (optional)

1 You can use the picture as an introduction to the Bible story or to help you review the story together.

2 Ask the children about their favourite foods. Who likes bananas, popcorn, raisins? You could play a game where the children stand up or sit down, as you call out different things to eat.

3 Say that the Bible story is about Daniel and his friends – and about what they wanted to eat. Look at the Bible story picture and let the children decorate the people standing around the table. (Daniel and his friends.) They could colour the food or stick on pictures of fruit and vegetables, from magazines.

4 Find out why Daniel and his friends ate these foods, in the Bible story.

For older children

Making prayer bracelets

25 *minutes*

Why: to remind the young people to do what God would want – regardless of what others around them do
With: embroidery thread or wool in different colours

1 Encourage the young people to pick out two colours of embroidery thread or wool. They should have five strands of one colour and just one strand of the second colour. (The numbers are dependent on the thickness of the thread but the idea is that the bracelet will be a majority of one colour with a small amount of the second colour.)

2 Help the young people to plait, twist or knot the threads into a bracelet. Various methods would work and instructions can be found in craft books or online.

3 Explain that these prayer bracelets remind us that there are times when we have to stand up for what we believe and do something different from the crowd. In a way, we have to be that one strand that is different from all the rest. Encourage the young people to wear the bracelets at school this week and to look at them when they are facing a situation where they need to 'stand out' and act as God would want them to.

4 Conclude by praying that God would help each person to know when and how to stand up for what they believe. Ask God to help the young people to be the 'different-coloured strand' for him.

THE LEARN AND REMEMBER VERSE

'He supplies the needs of those who honour him; he hears their cries and saves them.'

Psalm 145:19

Say that Daniel and his friends would have remembered what God wanted through the songs they learned as children. Use the Learn and remember song 'He supplies' (on the *Bitesize Bible Songs 2* CD, available from Scripture Union), or encourage children to make up their own song to these words.

Find a poster for this Learn and remember verse on page 90.

Use with **Bible story picture**
Daniel's new life Daniel 1

SERIES 4 DARING DANIEL

SESSION 2

Daniel in the lions' den

Bible:
Daniel 6

Aim: To be inspired to live for God even when it is not easy

CORE PROGRAMME

For 3 to 14s

Interview

(10) *minutes*

Why: to be inspired to live for God, even when it's not easy
With: a former or current mission partner or full-time Christian worker; or a simple biography

1 Before the visit, encourage the children to think of some questions they might like to ask. For example, how did the mission partner cope when things were difficult?

2 Invite your visitor to talk about the work they do for God and to show photos, if they have them.

3 Invite the children to pray for their visitor, asking God to help them with their work and keep them safe, particularly when things aren't easy.

4 If you have no suitable guest, read a short, simple biography of a missionary who has lived for God in difficult circumstances, such as Gladys Aylward, Jackie Pullinger, Mother Teresa, George Müller or Jim Elliot. Thank God for them.

Bible story with mime and sound effects

(15) - (20) *minutes*

Why: to be inspired to live for God even when it's not easy
With: SU *Bible Timeline* or the *Big Bible Storybook Timeline* (see page 96 for details) (optional)

1 **SU *Bible Timeline***
Ask the children to look along the *Bible Timeline* to see if they can find where Daniel is mentioned. Stop when you reach 'God punishes his people'. Ask them if they know a famous story about Daniel. Encourage them to practise roaring like lions and then, at a given signal, to shut their mouths. Practise several times until they get it right.

2 **Telling the story**
Ask questions to remind everyone about last session's Bible story. Explain that some years later there was a new king called Darius. In today's story they are going to hear about something very frightening that happened to Daniel.

Choose four children to be the king, Daniel and two jealous officials. The rest will be lions. Provide the king with a 'throne'. The Bible account is very straightforward, so it can be read straight from a child-friendly translation such as the Contemporary English Version, which is available online at www.biblegateway.com.

Read Daniel 6:1–5. Ask 'Daniel' to mime doing his work while the other two men whisper to each other. Ask the children whether they have any ideas about what the two men are plotting. (*They want to get Daniel into trouble.*)

Read verses 6–9. *(The officials mime going to the king, who then mimes writing his law.)* Ask the children what they think Daniel should do now, and why.

Read verses 10 and 11. *('Daniel' mimes praying; the two officials mime watching.)* Ask the children what they think will happen next.

Read verses 12–14. *(The officials mime going to the king; the king is thinking hard.)* Ask the children whether they think he will change his new law. Why not?

Read verses 15 and 16 *(ask the lions to roar)*, then read verses 17 and 18. *(The king mimes lying down but he is not able to sleep, he keeps turning over.)* Ask the children what they think will happen. *(Ask the lions to roar again, then signal to them to close their mouths.)*

Read verses 19 and 20. *(The king mimes hurrying to the pit, where the lions are lying down quietly.)*

Read verses 21–23. *(Daniel comes out of the pit.)* If you have time, read the story through again without stopping, with another four children playing the four roles.

3 **Think about**
Ask the children why Daniel was kept safe. Re-read verse 23b as a reminder. Ask the children what they think happened to the king. Read verses 25–27. Say that Daniel's faith and courage meant that the king believed in God too, and wanted everyone in the country to worship him.

4 **Response**
Discuss whether it was easy for Daniel to disobey the king's new law. Explain that in some countries today it is against the law to worship God. In some countries people have to decide whether to obey God or to obey their rulers; sometimes people are put in prison for worshipping God. (Make sure you do not frighten the children.) Reassure them that in most Western countries people are allowed to worship God and they are unlikely to have to make difficult choices like Daniel did. However, say that they may sometimes have to make difficult choices about how they should behave. Say a prayer, asking God to help the children (and leaders!) to live for God like Daniel.

Prayer walk

(10) *minutes*

Why: to be inspired to live for God by encouraging prayer
With: extra supervision

1 Read Daniel 6:26,27 and challenge the children to guess who originally spoke the words. It wasn't Daniel, but King Darius, who learned about living for God when he was older.

2 Practise saying the words of this response, aloud in two parts:

A: He is the living God...
B: ... the one who lives for ever.
A: His power and his kingdom...
B: ... will never end.
All: He rescues people and sets them free by working great miracles!

3 Walk with the children to two or three safe places around your church building or meeting place and say the prayer aloud. Encourage the children to say this prayer (or their own prayers), asking God to help your church members of all ages to keep living for God.

PHOTOCOPIABLE PART

Picture for use with **Lions' den**

CORE PROGRAMME CONTINUED

Scoring game

(5) - (10) minutes

Why: to think about things we find easy or hard

1 Give out pens and paper and invite each child to make ten small scorecards, one for each of the numbers zero to nine.

2 Mention some things they might be asked to do: sums, swimming, praying or doing what they're told. Ask them to hold up a score on how difficult it is: zero is 'easy-peasy' and ten is 'impossibly difficult'. Use their scores to chat about why some things are difficult.

3 Explain that they can't all be brilliant at sums or football, but that God will always help them to do the things he wants.

Bible story picture

(5) - (10) minutes

Why: to realise that we can talk to God in any situation
With: a copy of the picture from page 89 (printed on A4 paper) for each child or enlarged copies for group use, art and craft materials

1 You can use the picture as an introduction to the Bible story or to help you review the story together.

2 Describe how Daniel always prayed to God – and how men who did not like him got the king to put him in with the lions! These were not cuddly toy lions or plastic models – these were big, hungry lions with lots of teeth!

3 Ask the children what they think happened next. (Be prepared for gruesome details!)

4 Then look at the Bible story picture to see what really happened: the lions did not hurt Daniel at all because God stopped them!

EXTENSION IDEAS

Activities for younger children

Thank-you song

(10) minutes

Why: to thank God for always being with us

1 Ask the children to call out places they go during a typical day. Ask who is there with them. To the tune of 'Frère Jacques', sing the following, changing the first line according to the children's suggestions:

When I'm at school,
when I'm at school (...in bed/ ...playing/ ...frightened)
You're there too.
You're there too.
You are always with me.
You are always with me.
Thank you, God.
Thank you, God.

2 After several verses, say that today you are finding out that God was with Daniel in a very strange place. (If you have already heard the Bible story, see if the children can tell you about that 'strange place'.)

For older children

Lions' den

(10) minutes

Why: to be inspired to live for God even when it's not easy
With: paper, roughly A6 size; lions from page 87

1 Encourage the children to think about places or situations when it isn't easy to live for God. Encourage them to write each of these on a lion shape, cut it out and place it on the floor to form a den of lions.

2 Give each child a smaller piece of paper and invite them to draw themselves, cut it out and place it in the 'den', in the middle of the lions.

3 Read some of the words written on the lions. Say that Daniel's life was full of prayer, even when facing lions. Help the children to pray for each other to live for God in their everyday situations. As the children pray, turn the lions around, facing away from the 'people'.

THE LEARN AND REMEMBER VERSE

'He supplies / the needs / of those who honour him; / he hears / their cries / and saves them.' / Psalm 145:19

Write the verse in sections (as above) on seven large sheets of card. Display them at random around the room. Read the verse slowly, and invite the children to run from one section to the next. Repeat. Finally, challenge the children to collect all the sections and rearrange them in order. Talk about how this verse was true for Daniel and how it can be true for us too.

Find a poster for this Learn and remember verse on page 90.

You could also use the song 'He supplies', on the *Bitesize Bible Songs 2* CD, available from Scripture Union.

Use with **Bible story picture**
Daniel prays to God Daniel 6

'He supplies the needs of those who honour him; he hears their cries and saves them.'

Psalm 145:19

ALL-AGE SERVICE

Turning up the heat!

Readings:
Daniel 3; Isaiah 43:1–7; Exodus 20:4–6

Aim: To help people stand up for God even when it is tough

GETTING STARTED

It must have been a terrifying moment for the three young men standing in front of the blazing furnace... the smoke rising and the heat building! The pressure is on!

They could have talked themselves out of it, saying, 'Well, we could just bow down once. What harm could it do? We wouldn't really be actually "worshipping" the statue in our hearts would we?'

But they chose to do no such thing. They remembered the commandment God had spoken, 'You shall not make for yourself an idol. ... You shall not bow down to them or worship them' (Exodus 20:4-6). And they decided that they must obey God, rather than fear man.

A decision to stand up for what we know is right can be tough. Plenty of things can get in the way to distract us from 'walking into the flames'.

The material for this service explores some of these themes. We pray that you grasp something pertinent and timely, for yourself, and for your congregation here.

YOU WILL NEED

- 'Bow down and worship him' mp3 which you can download at www.mp3s.pl/mp3/Ben_Cantelon/Bow_Down_And_Worship_Him/2028828 for **Beginning the service**
- play money, cardboard flames, cardboard statue, crown, white outfit, piece of music from a CD or instrument for **Bible reading**
- loud music from a CD or instrument, mobile phone, for **Prayer activity**
- sticky notes for **Prayers of confession**
- five obstacles such as a chair, a pile of books, a person lying down, a suitcase, a couple of shopping bags; five large labels with the Bible verses written on; sticky tape for **Game**

BEGINNING THE SERVICE

As people are coming in, play 'Bow down and worship him' by Ben Cantelon.

When the service leader starts to welcome everyone and introduce the theme, ask the person's wife/husband or best friend to come up and stand beside them. The service leader acts surprised and asks what they are doing. The person says, 'I am standing with you.'

The service leader gives them a funny look, and then carries on, perhaps giving out a notice or commenting on the weather. Again they stop and say, 'What did you say you were doing here?'

The person simply replies again, 'I am standing with you.'

The service leader again introduces the theme of the service saying that the story is all about three men who chose to stand up for what they believed and, in doing so, witnessed a miracle and were saved from the flames.

At the end, they turn to the person one more time and ask, 'Why are you here?'

The person simply says, 'I am standing with you. Just like Jesus stands with us.'

Light dawns for the service leader who then introduces the Bible reading below, saying, 'Oh... I get it! Well, to see what they meant, let's hear this.'

BIBLE READING

With: script, play money, cardboard flames, a cardboard statue, a crown for the king, white outfit for the angel and a loud piece of music either from a CD or instrument

You will need a narrator, king and angel. The king and angel are 'non-speaking' parts. You will also need volunteers from the congregation to play the important people of the land, the three men, the soldiers and a helper to bring out the statue.

Part way through the script, the king needs to select members of the congregation to play various roles. While the roles are simple and the required actions obvious, you may like to pre-select some helpers you can rely on! The roles of Shadrach, Meshach and Abednego can be played by three children from the congregation.

You will need to make a couple of props to bring the story to life. These are merely there to give a visual aid to your retelling. To make the cardboard flames cut one or two pieces of card into flame shapes and paint them orange, yellow and red. To make the statue, place three or four cardboard boxes on top of one another, secure them with tape or PVA glue and either paint them gold or cover them with gold wrapping paper.

Narrator: There was once a king with a VERY long name. He was called Nebunoozer, no sorry, Nebuwhooser, no that's not right, Nebuchadnezzar. We'll call him King Neb.

King Neb stands at the front with crown on and gives a royal wave.

Narrator: King Neb had LOADS of money.

King Neb fans play money around.

Narrator: He used to sit around in his palace all day wondering what he could with it. Should he use it to sleep on instead of a pillow?

King Neb puts money in both hands and places head on it.

Narrator: Should he wear it instead of clothes?

King Neb tries to pin it to clothing.

Narrator: Or should he use it to fan himself with when he got hot?

King Neb fans himself with notes.

Narrator: No, these were all silly ideas so King Neb kept thinking.

King Neb taps his head and looks thoughtful.

Narrator: One day, he had an idea.

King Neb jumps up and shouts, 'Eureka!'

Narrator: King Neb decided to build an enormous statue made of pure gold. It was over 27 metres high and almost 3 metres wide and he set it on the plain of Dura in Babylon.

Helpers bring out the statue. King Neb directs the helpers as to where to put it.

Narrator: He was SO excited about his statue that the king called all the important people of the land to see it.

King Neb selects people from the congregation to come and look.

Narrator: They all 'oohhed' and 'aahhed' and admired the king's lovely statue.

Important people say 'Ooh' and 'aah'.

Narrator: King Neb was really pleased with his statue. In fact, he was so pleased that he decided every time his favourite music was played all the people of the land must immediately fall to the ground and worship his statue. Anyone who did not obey the king would be thrown into a blazing fire.

Play music. The important people fall to the ground.

Narrator: King Neb enjoyed watching the people obey him. So he played his music quite often.

Play music a couple more times. King Neb looks gleeful. The important people fall to the ground each time.

Narrator: Now, there were three men called Shadrach, Meshach and Abednego who worked for the king.

Three children to come to the front to play the three men.

Narrator: These men loved God and whenever the music played they refused to bow down to the huge gold statue.

The three men shake their heads.

Narrator: This made King Neb VERY angry. He called the men before him and demanded that they bow to the statue or be thrown into the fire.

King Neb looks angry and calls the children over. He points to the statue and then the floor.

Narrator: Shadrach, Meshach and Abednego shook their heads and crossed their arms.

The three men shake their heads and cross their arms.

Narrator: 'No way, King Neb! We serve God, not your statue. We're not scared of your fire. The God we serve is able to save us,' they said.

This made King Neb VERY, VERY angry. He ordered that the fire should be hotter than it had ever been before, seven times hotter in fact, and commanded that the strongest soldiers in his army tie Shadrach, Meshach and Abednego up and throw them in.

King Neb looks angry, points to the flames and raises his arms to signify heating up the furnace. Select someone from the congregation to push the three into the fire. The three men hide behind the flames.

Narrator: The king rubbed his hands in glee and went over to warm himself by the fire.

King Neb stands in front of the fire and rubs his hands in glee.

Narrator: Hey, wait a minute. The king has turned a funny colour. He's pointing at something. What is he looking at?

King Neb looks astonished and points to the flames.

Narrator: There are four men walking around. Shadrach, Meshach, Abednego and a man dressed in white. He looks remarkably like an angel.

The three men and the angel stand up and hold hands.

Narrator: King Neb went to the opening of the blaze and ordered the men to come out.

King Neb cups his hands around his mouth and signals for the men to come out. The angel leaves the stage.

Narrator: King Neb looked astounded. The fire had not harmed them one little bit. There was no smoky bonfire smell, no frayed clothing, not even a hair on their heads had been singed.

King Neb inspects the three children, sniffs them, picks at their clothes and holds up their hair.

Narrator: King Neb was amazed and for once he saw things as they were.

King Neb rubs his eyes.

Narrator: He realised that the three men worshipped a real God who had protected them and saved them from harm. He shook their hands and made a new declaration. He said that from this moment on no one was to speak badly about Shadrach, Meshach and Abednego's God. For the God they served truly had saved them.

King Neb shakes the children's hands. They cheer and hold up their hands.

BIBLE TALK

With: animated version of the Bible story such as this toy-figure retelling at www.youtube.com/watch?v=JaigJIQDVvE&feature=related

Show the video clip and then say the following:

Sometimes we have bad days, don't we?

Maybe things go wrong at work or school, or we argue as a family. Sometimes it's hard to remember that God is there with us through those things, isn't it? (Show the words of the Learn and remember verse (poster on page 90): 'He supplies the needs of those who honour him; he hears their cries and saves them.' Psalm 145:19).

Continue: Daniel 3:17 says this, '... the God we worship can save us ...'

Can we say that all together? '... the God we worship can save us ...'

The three men in our story could have seen this experience as the worst day ever! But it turned out to be probably the best day of their lives!

How and why?

Because they said this to themselves and to the king: 'The God we worship can save us!'

What kinds of things make us scared?

Perhaps ask the congregation with a roving mic and get others in the congregation to raise their hand if they are scared of that thing.

What difference does it make to us to know that the God we serve is able to save us, not necessarily from those things, but from the FEAR of those things?

Bad days become the BEST days ever when we know this to be true. We can conquer our fears when we know that God stands with us in the midst of it all.

So what can we learn from this story?

- The men knew God well. They weren't distracted by the heat or the angry king. We need to know God well and know how to act in every circumstance.
- Their faith was based on who God is. Not if he would save them or not. Our faith should be based on this too.
- They walked into the fire and met with God himself. When we experience trouble God will be there too.

Nebuchadnezzar came as close as he could to the furnace and shouted in the doorway, 'You servants of the Most High God, come out at once!'

Now remember Nebuchadnezzar has set up a statue that showed he thought he was the Most High God around. But what he saw in the fire changed his mind.

Bad days can turn into the best days ever if we can truly say 'the God we worship can save us!' They can also change the minds of people around us too. Let us say that one more time... 'The God we worship can save us!'

PRAYER ACTIVITY

Tell the congregation that you are now going to pray. Wait until there is quiet and then play some very loud music. As people look up, turn the music off, and apologise for the distraction.

Start to pray again... A mobile phone rings and someone is talking on it very loudly. Again apologise.

Start to pray again... Arrange for someone to start poking, prodding and dancing in front of you.

Talk about how modern life is busy and noisy and we are very easily distracted. Talk about the benefits of turning off the TV, the radio, the Internet and our mobile phones and going to a place where we can be alone with God, even if it's only for a few minutes.

Encourage quiet for one minute. In the quietness, encourage people to listen and speak to God. After the minute of quiet, pray that the congregation will learn not to be distracted by the busyness of modern life and to tune into God.

PRAYERS OF CONFESSION

With: sticky notes, cardboard statue from **Bible reading**

Ask the congregation to think about the things that they are tempted to bow down to in place of God. Give examples such as football, money, work, pop idols and so on. Talk about how God wants to be number one in our lives and that we should be most concerned with pleasing him. Explain that, like the three men in the story, we need to refuse to bow down to anything else.

Hand out the sticky notes. Ask the congregation to write down the things that they are tempted to bow down to. Once they have done this ask them to stick their notes on the cardboard statue used in the Bible reading. As they do so, ask them to seek forgiveness from God for the things that they have put in his place. Encourage them to pray for God's help in restoring the correct priorities in their lives.

ENDING THE SERVICE

Remind everyone that the three men in the story did not shy away from standing up for God. God not only saved them from the burning flames but he also stood in there with them! No matter what our situation, God will always stand alongside and reward those who know him, trust him and speak up for him. Remind everyone that God is able to save them from any fear, or help them conquer any distraction.

HELPFUL EXTRAS

Music and song ideas

- 'Our God is a great big God' (*Songs of Fellowship 2004*)
- 'We bow down and confess' (*Songs of Fellowship 1084*)
- 'Stand up, stand up for Jesus' (*Songs of Fellowship 513*)

Game

With: five 'obstacles' such as a chair, a pile of books, a person lying down, a suitcase, a couple of shopping bags; a Bible verse attached to each item, sticky tape

Set up an obstacle race in the church with two adult or youth competitors. There need to be at least five things they must overcome. Each of the items has a Bible verse attached to it with sticky tape. As they seek to get over each obstacle, they must shout out the Bible passage attached to each one.

At the end state that the winner was not the one that came first, but the one who took time to read truth every time they met an obstacle.

Suggested Bible verses for the game:

- '... the God we worship can save us ...' Daniel 3:17
- 'Don't be afraid, I have rescued you. I have called you by name, now you belong to me.' Isaiah 43:1
- 'When you cross deep rivers, I will be with you and you won't drown.' Isaiah 43:2
- 'When you walk through fire, you won't be burnt or scorched by the flames.' Isaiah 43:3
- 'Don't be afraid! I am with you.' Isaiah 43:5

NOTES AND COMMENTS

An alternative prayer activity could be to set up areas around the room to represent the places where the congregation spend their time, for example, school, workplace, home and community. Encourage the congregation to think about which area they spend the most time in and ask them to go to it. In the small groups ask people to pray for one another that they will learn to be ambassadors for Jesus, unafraid to stand up for him in their schools, workplaces, homes and communities. You might like to place some youth and children's workers in the school corner to help pray for the young people.

Service written by Ems Hancock and Sian Ashford

MOSAIC BOOKSHELF

Scripture Union's *Bible Timelines* have helped thousands of children get to know the big story of the Bible - God's great plan for salvation - for many years now. Each colourful and informative version (for young children, older children and young people) takes you through the big story of the Bible from Creation to Revelation, in 16 illustrated panels. Choose one, or more, to introduce the children in your small group to God's big picture.

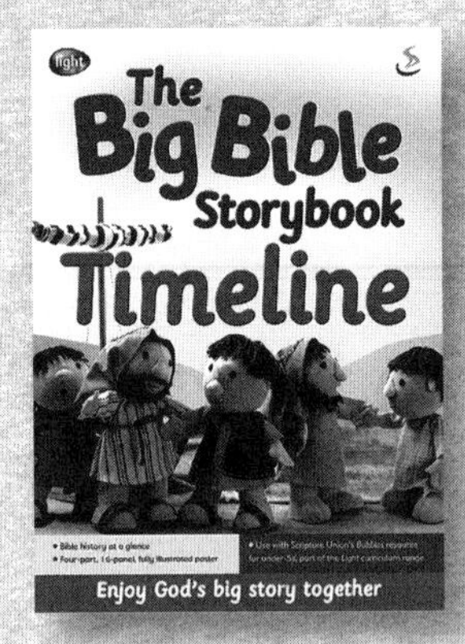

The Big Bible Storybook Timeline

£11.99 ISBN 978 1 84427 361 4

Does the story of Moses come before or after David, in the Bible? Was Paul around at the same time as Jesus? For most of us, Bible reading, teaching or sermons happen piecemeal - a verse here, a chapter there, maybe a complete letter or a short book. The *Big Bible Storybook Timeline* is here to help you see God's big story in its historical order.

The pack contains the four-part illustrated *Big Bible Storybook Timeline* poster with adhesive strips, ready to be joined together, together with suggestions for activities to use with children.

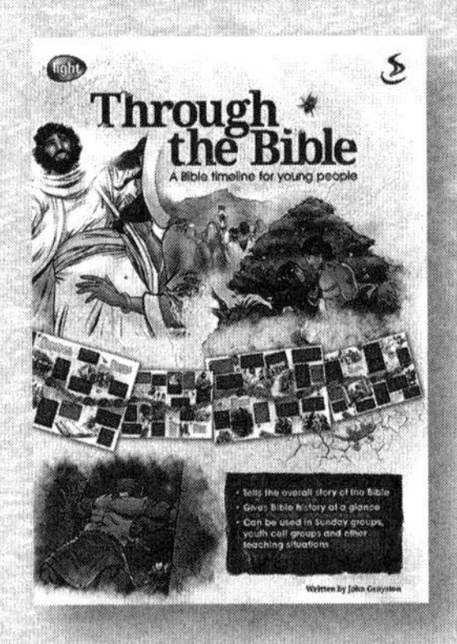

Through the Bible

Youth Timeline - A Bible Timeline for Young People (new and updated version)

£11.99 ISBN 978 1 84427 644 8

To young people, the Bible can appear dull, complicated or irrelevant. *Through the Bible* sets out to dispel those preconceptions. This timeline helps young people and their leaders discover more about some of the main characters in the Bible, and build their understanding of the big themes, such as sin, covenant and prophecy. These themes form a framework on which young people can hang the individual stories they encounter.

Made of four separate pieces, the timeline can be joined together into one long poster to be displayed in a church or youth group setting; or kept in its folder and brought out when needed, if display facilities are limited.

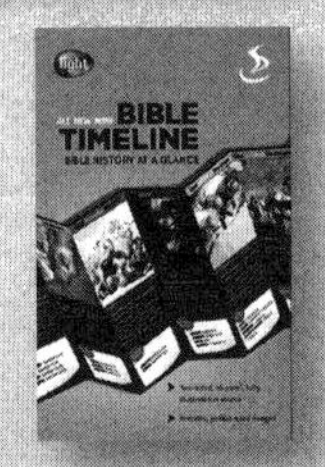

Bible Timeline

(new and updated version)

£11.99 ISBN 978 1 84427 643 1

What's the big story all about? Scripture Union's *Bible Timeline* will help you answer this question, at a glance. The 16 panels each illustrate a key person or event in Bible history. Underneath each picture, key dates and characters are highlighted. Bible references will help you locate the stories in the Bible quickly and easily.

The pack contains the four-part illustrated *Bible Timeline* poster with adhesive strips, ready to be joined together, together with ideas to help you make the most of your *Bible Timeline*.

Mini Bible Timeline

75p ISBN 978 1 84427 729 2

This new *Mini Bible Timeline* has been produced to complement its larger counterpart. The story of the Old Testament appears on one side of this fold-up pocket guide, while the New Testament story is on the other. Using engaging artwork and text, this retelling of the Bible story will be useful for leaders and makes a great gift for the children in your group.

Mini Bible Timeline (10 pack)

£4.99 ISBN 978 1 84427 730 8

This multi-buy offer makes the *Mini Bible Timeline* even more affordable.Why not buy a set and give one to each child in your group?